A New View of Society

A New View of Society

OR

ESSAYS

ON THE FORMATION

OF THE

HUMAN CHARACTER

Preparatory to the Developement of a Plan for
gradually ameliorating the Condition of

MANKIND

BY

ROBERT OWEN

[1816]

WITH AN INTRODUCTION BY
JOHN SAVILLE

MACMILLAN

Introduction © John Saville 1972

First Edition 1813

First Edition in Book Form 1816

(London: *Printed for* Longman, Hurst, Rees, Orme
& Brown, *Pater-noster Row*; Cadell & Davies, *Strand*;
J. Hatchard, *Piccadilly*; J. Murray, *Albemarle-Street*;
Constable & Co. and Oliphant & Co , *Edinburgh*: Smith
& Sons and Brash & Reid, *Glasgow*; and sold by all
the Booksellers in town and country.)

This edition published 1972 by
THE MACMILLAN PRESS LTD
London and Basingstoke
Associated companies in New York Toronto
Dublin Melbourne Johannesburg and Madras

SBN 333 14243 8

Printed in the United States of America by
Sentry Press, New York, N. Y., 10013

INTRODUCTION

Robert Owen was born in 1771 in Newtown, Montgomeryshire, a remote part of central Wales. His father was a saddler and ironmonger who was also the local postmaster. Robert, who was not a robust child, showed early signs of a considerable intellectual development, and at the age of seven was already being used to teach other boys in the local school. At the age of nine he began his first job, and a year later left his family to work for three years as an apprentice to a draper in Stamford, in Lincolnshire, one of the eastern counties of England. He later moved to London and then to Manchester; and at the age of eighteen, in this latter town, he set up in business, with a partner, making spinning machines. The venture was not a success but two years later Owen, now twenty, commenced business on his own account as a master cotton-spinner, employing three men to work five spinning mules. This was the beginning of his notable achievement as a business man, and before the year was out he had become manager of a mill, owned by a Mr. Drinkwater, which employed 500 men.[1]

Owen's extraordinary early career as a business man was told in great detail in his own autobiography, written and published at the end of his life. From his earliest days he seems to have exhibited the characteristics of personal gentleness, equability of temperament, and general reasonableness, which always remained with him. In particular he appeared to be able to exercise a quite remarkable influence and persuasiveness over those with whom he made social contact.[2] The business world

iii

in Manchester in which he found himself in his late teens
and early manhood was an interesting testing ground for
his qualities and abilities. The town was at the centre
of the rapid industrial and commercial changes that had
begun to transform the economic and social structure of
Britain from the late decades of the eighteenth century.
Cotton manufacture, the most technically advanced of
all industries, was growing at an extraordinary rate and
factories, the symbols of the new industrial age, were
being built in large numbers. Manchester and its surrounding towns were growing fast in population; the
intensity of exploitation of the early generations of cotton workers was notorious, and the rate of profit to be
gained by enterprising entrepreneurs was correspond-
ingly high. By the time Owen left Manchester at the
end of the 1790's he was already prosperous and his
knowledge of techniques and management problems in
the cotton industry very advanced.

Owen's intellectual development during his Manchester years is not as fully documented as we could
wish. He was invited to join and take part in the discussion of the Literary and Philosophical Society, the
centre of Manchester's intellectual life, and he also became involved in Manchester College.[3] His nickname
at the latter institution was 'the reasoning machine',
his main intellectual interest already being the development of society on rational lines through a thorough-
going system of education. He certainly read William
Godwin's *Political Justice,* a book which was to influence his thinking considerably in the future, but he
came to have a poor opinion of books in his later life
and this is probably the reason why there is so little
mention of them in his own autobiography. At the end
of his first decade as a cotton manufacturer he bought

from David Dale the famous New Lanark mills, the best equipped as well as the largest spinning mills in Scotland; and for the next few years after 1800 he was busily engaged in transforming them into a model factory enterprise as well as a highly profitable one.[4] The management problems and especially the labour problems he faced at New Lanark were common to all the early generations of entrepreneurs in industrial Britain; and Owen solved them in interesting and imaginative ways. He was always paternalistic—a characteristic which remained with him throughout his life—but he was possessed above all with a profound concern for people. The employment of pauper children revolted him and the use of any child below the age of ten was not to be tolerated; and after cleaning up and greatly improving the physical environment in which his workers lived, and reorganizing the internal organisation and work flow of the New Lanark mills,[5] Owen then set about providing educational facilities, and developing new ideas about educational techniques, which were to make New Lanark a centre of pilgrimage for over two decades. It was these educational experiments and practices that were to lead to the publication of his first major work, the *New View of Society*, the first essay of which appeared in 1813.

At the time he was writing the first part of the *New View*, Owen was involved in a crisis with his business partners from which he extricated himself by arranging a partnership with a new group which brought him the financial support of a number of more eminent people than those with whom he had previously been associated; and one result was that he was able to develop his educational ideas still further. In 1814 he began to build the famous Institute for the Formation of Character.

The Institute included a school for the children who worked at the factory, community rooms for adults and a 'playground', that is, a nursery school, for infants and young children. It was the Institute, and especially the provision for nursery education, that brought the astonishing number of visitors each year to New Lanark.[6] For Owen the education given to children must be natural, spontaneous and enjoyable: characteristics which were to be in very short supply in the British educational system until well into the twentieth century. Books were used chiefly for reference purposes; the children engaged in a great deal of physical exercise, including dancing; music and singing were practised from the earliest age-groups. By nineteenth century standards the educational regimen was extraordinarily liberal; and nowhere was this more marked than at the nursery stage.

In Owen's approach there was much that had already been discussed by earlier writers of the Enlightenment, among them Rousseau and Helvétius and among his own generation, Godwin. Whether Owen had ever read Rousseau is not known, but it is unlikely, and he did not meet Pestallozzi, Rousseau's educational disciple, until his continental tour of 1818. Much that he was to say, then, in the *New View* was to be found, often in a more sophisticated form, in earlier works. As with Helvétius education for Owen meant total education, the reshaping of the child and later the man 'in good habits of every description.'[7] What needs, however, to be emphasised about the *New View* is not only the restatement of arguments previously propounded—this has always been understood—but rather the tone in which Owen's thinking was phrased. For Owen was writing from within the new industrial system; this was his

starting point and what he was saying related directly
to his own experience within the new environment of
the factory and child labour. A good deal of the argument in the *New View* was conservative in its implica-
tions, but to emphasise the traditional context in which
certain arguments were developed and to miss the
humanitarianism derived from a close working experience of the new industrialist society is to fail to comprehend the development of Owen's later thought and
practice. The rationalist educator of the *New View*
became in a few years the millenial communitarian of
the *Report of the County of Lanark,* and to understand
how the one developed from the other requires an ap-
preciation of the *New View* as the seed-bed of what was
to show itself later. Owen remained a rationalist educator all his life, and many of his later ideas were a logical
extension of the educational theories first expressed at
length in the *New View of Society.*

The First Essay was a statement of general principles.
It began with the recognition that some three-fourths of
the total population of Britain were working class; that
the existing arrangements of society encouraged 'extreme vice and misery' among many and for the rest
produced a general conduct of society totally unworthy
of rational beings.[8] His central argument was the
familiar one of individual character moulded by the
environment in which the individual lived. He accepted
this as axiomatic, noting that

> it cannot now be necessary to enter into the detail
> of facts to prove that children can be trained to
> acquire *'any language, sentiments, belief, or any
> bodily habits and manners, not contrary to human
> nature.'*

The way out for 'poor traduced and degraded human nature' was straightforward and simple, for there was no conflict between 'the happiness of self' and 'the happiness of the community.'[9] What was needed— indeed all that was required—was the education and training of children 'from their earliest infancy' in the principles and practices of a rational education; the product of which could only be the 'active and ardent desire to promote the happiness of every individual' in society. Society had spent millions on the detection and punishment of crimes, and 'yet we have not moved one step in the true path to *prevent* crimes, and to diminish the innumerable evils with which mankind are now afflicted.'

The First Essay was a statement then of general ideas; and in the Second Essay, after restating his basic principles once again,[10] Owen then set forth the educational and social ideas which informed his administration of the community at New Lanark. It included a rejection of sectarian religion and an argument for toleration among the sects in a comment which presaged Owen's later much more vigorous attack upon the practices of the established religious churches. He insisted that his ideas, having been shown to be fully practicable, could be extended to the whole of British society; that such an application of a rational educational system could be made without 'the least danger to any individual or to any part of society'; and his argument throughout is shot through with the conviction that once members of the government and the leaders of society grasped his ideas, they would immediately see their central importance and significance for the future well-being of the millions over whom they had control. Owen was convinced at this time, and in a

crucial sense remained convinced all his life, that the
self-interest of legislators would lead them to a rational
solution of the problems of society. Once they understood, they would act.

The Third Essay took the general argument and
description of the New Lanark experiment further, and
in particular Owen discussed the principles upon which
the 'New Institution,' that is, the Institution for the
Formation of Character, were founded. The importance
of 'happiness' was a constantly re-iterated theme of
Owen's writing, and in this Third Essay he insisted
upon 'the careful provision' for amusement and recreation for everyone. 'The Sabbath' he wrote 'was originally so intended'; and he then proceeded to attack the
joyless Sundays which the various religious sects had
imposed upon the people. Throughout the *New View*
we are constantly reminded of the conditions upon
which the good life may be founded. Far too much has
been made by many of Owen's critics of the repetitive-
ness of his writing, of his constant harping upon his
central idea that 'the character of man is, without a
single exception, always formed for him'; and what is
too often missed is the profound humanism that pervades his ideas and his writings.[11] In the immediate
aftermath of the Napoleonic Wars such ideas were
sharply at variance with established opinion, and it was
only the meandering gentleness of Owen's exposition,
together with his belief that what he was proposing
would in no way disturb the existing social relations of
society, that won him temporarily the support of the
Establishment of the day. When he moved beyond the
propositions advanced in the *New View* to a sharper
statement of both his ideas and solutions for contem-

porary problems, the verbal expression of support quickly turned into outright hostility.

In the Fourth, and last Essay, Owen offered some suggestions for government action along the lines of his general principles. He began with an old-fashioned statement concerning the purposes of government, one which accorded with his paternalism:

> The end of government is to make the governed and the governors happy.
>
> That government then is the best, which in practice produces the greatest happiness to the greatest number; including those who govern, and those who obey.

Owen's philosophic ideas were of a mechanical materialist kind; the word 'train' as applied to the inculcation of correct ideas in children and adults is constantly used and his theory of man's character being entirely derived from the circumstances of his upbringing allowed no room for active reflection and a positive reshaping of ideas within individual man. Yet his imagination at least partly denied his passive theories, and in his insistence upon the creativeness of infant and child education, he was going beyond his own theories. In this Fourth Essay for example, he now criticized the educational systems of Bell and Lancaster, whereas in the First Essay he had commended them as 'among the most important benefactors of the human race.' The extent to which Owen in these post-1815 years was modifying and enlarging his ideas has often been seriously underestimated, and a quite wrong impression has been given of him as 'a man with one idea' which he repeated *ad nauseam*.

His practical proposals in the final essay listed first, the establishment of a national system of education, with appropriate institutions, including the training of teachers, all under the control of a new department of government, 'which will be found ultimately to prove the most important of all its departments' (p. 167); and then there followed a series of interesting proposals which were not in any way related to any of the previous discussion in the *New View* but referred to Owen's concern with the problems of the post-war world with which he was from this time to be increasingly involved. In the *New View* (p. 170) he referred briefly to the problem of employment and suggested that what was first needed was 'regular and accurate information relative to the value of and demand for labour.' His practical proposals were eminently sensible and were not to be achieved until the twentieth century.

He concluded the Fourth Essay by appealing once again to the legislators; by emphasising that 'with all its errors' the British government was among the 'most enlightened' that the world had yet seen; and by reiterating how straightforward and simple his principles were in terms of their application to the whole nation.

* * *

In the years between the appearance of the First Essay of the *New View* in 1813 and publication of the *Report to the County of Lanark* in 1820, Owen responded to the problems and difficulties of post-war society by a remarkable enlargement of his intellectual horizons. In the *New View* he emerged as a rational educator and psychologist, but he now began to concern himself with the problems of child labour in the expanding industrial system, and, just as important, with the new phenomenon of large-scale unemployment. As he wrote in a striking paragraph in his autobiography: 'The war was a great and most extravagant customer to farmers, manufacturers, and other producers of wealth, and many during this period became very wealthy. . . . And on the day on which peace was signed, this great customer of the producers died, and prices fell as the demand diminished. . .'.[12] In the *Observations on the Effect of the Manufacturing System,* published in 1815, and in a number of subsequent speeches, addresses and pamphlets, Owen began to explore the nature of the new industrial society, the causes of its degrading effects upon the working people, the solutions to the problem of unemployment and the large-scale remedies that were required. He still addressed himself, in the years immediately after 1815, to those in power; the title page of the *Observations* is 'Dedicated most Respectfully to the British Legislature'; and so long as he couched his own opinion in generalised forms he continued to evoke a response from those to whom he looked for a practical remedy to the evils he was describing. It was his famous attack in 1817 on 'the errors—gross errors—that have been combined with the fundamental notions of every religion that has hitherto been taught to men'[13] together with the advocacy of villages of co-operation that brought swiftly to an end the encomiums hitherto lavished upon him. Owen, the socialist, was born in these years and the *Report to the County of Lanark* sums up the intellectual journeying of the previous half-dozen years.

What must be insisted upon is Owen's originality. He emphasised the tremendous productive powers now available to mankind following on the invention of the steam engine and the new technology; he recognised the

existence of technological unemployment; and he ana-
lysed the economic problem of unemployment in terms
of a deficiency of demand and argued a vigorous case
for 'the economy of high wages.' He deepened his
critique of industrial society by emphasising the fundamental contradiction between 'the principle of individual interest', celebrated by philosophers and econo-
mists, on the one hand, and the public good on the other;
and his words were to be echoed by every generation
of socialists who followed him:

> Under the present system there is the most minute
> division of mental power and manual labour in the
> individuals of the working classes; private interests
> are placed perpetually at variance with the public
> good; and in every nation men are purposely
> trained from infancy to suppose that their well-
> being is incompatible with the progress and pros-
> perity of other nations. Such are the means by which
> old society seeks to obtain the desired objects of
> life. The details now to be submitted have been
> devised upon principles which will lead to an op-
> posite practice; to the combination of extensive
> mental and manual powers in the individuals of the
> working classes; to a complete identity of private
> and public interest; and to the training of nations
> to comprehend that their power and happiness can-
> not attain their full and natural development but
> through an equal increase of the power and happi-
> ness of all other states.[14]

and again:

> From this principle of individual interest have
> arisen all the divisions of mankind, the endless

errors and mischiefs of class, sect, party, and of
national antipathies, creating the angry and male-
volent passions, and all the crimes and misery with
which the human race have been hitherto afflicted. [15]

It was this understanding of the basic conflict between
individual interest and the public good which led him
to the ideas of community. Originally his villages were
to be an answer to the post-war unemployment problem,
but by the time the 1820 *Report* was written, he had
understood their wider significance in terms of trans-
formation of existing society.

It is common among commentators on Robert Owen to
emphasise the utopianism of his approach to social questions, and the millenial cast to his thinking; to dwell
upon his political naivety and his refusal to comprehend
in any way the role of politics in social change; and to
underline how little he understood of the class structure
of society. A critique along these lines is fair comment
as is the general point that the ideas of Robert Owen
and the movement of Owenism after 1820 must be
clearly distinguished. Owenism had many facets, and
E. P. Thompson, among others, is right to stress that
those who followed Owen in the next three decades took
from him what related to their own experience, and
rejected what they found alien. [16] But when all is said,
Owen remains a thinker of great originality, a man of
imagination, a humanist who started from the premises
of an industrial society; in short, a contemporary thinker
of insight and relevance. That there was much dross
mixed with the creative grain of his thought is indisput-
able; and that in practical politics he was nearly always
a disastrous leader is again not in dispute. But no one
can take from Owen the insights he offered into the

working class condition or the vision of a just community that continued to excite and inspire many generations to come. He stands at the beginning of the modern socialist tradition in British life; his international influence in Europe and America was to be considerable; and his ideas continuously evoked a response and a reaction in the decades that followed the extraordinarily creative period of his thinking and writing that began with the *New View* in 1813 and culminated in the publication of the *Report to the County of Lanark* half a decade later.

The University,
Hull.
November 1971.

JOHN SAVILLE

NOTES

(1) The starting point for Owen's career is The *Life of Robert Owen, Written by Himself* (London, 1857; reprinted Kelley: New York, 1967). The volume covers Owen's life down to about 1820. The first scholarly work on Owen, and still a standard source, was Frank Podmore's two volume *Robert Owen: A Biography* (London, 1906; reprinted in one volume, Kelley: New York, 1968). G. D. H. Cole, *Robert Owen* (London, 1925) is a useful complement to Podmore, and Margaret Cole's *Robert Owen of New Lanark* (London, 1953) is a good short introduction to his life and work. The most important book on the Owenite movement as a whole is J. F. C. Harrison's *Robert Owen and the Owenities in Britain and America* (London, 1969) with a superb bibliography. A bi-centenary volume, *Robert Owen, Prophet of the Poor* (ed. by Sidney Pollard and John Salt, London, 1971) is a collection of essays on both Owen and the Owenite movement; and see also *Robert Owen and his Relevance to Our Times* (Co-operative College Papers, Loughborough, 1971) esp. Sidney Pollard, 'Robert Owen as an Economist,' pp. 23-36.

(2) Phrenologists were generally agreed that Robert Owen's bump of benevolence was unusually developed. George Combe reported on Owen's head in the *Phrenological Journal* (1823-1824) pp. 235-237; and see also Margaret Cole, 'Owen's Mind and Methods,' in *Robert Owen, Prophet of the Poor, op. cit.,* esp. p. 193 ff.

(3) *The Life of Robert Owen, Written by Himself,* p. 35 ff; and Podmore, *op. cit.,* ch. 3, 'Life in Manchester.'

(4) David Dale, whose daughter Caroline Owen was to marry about the same time as the purchase of the New Lanark mills was arranged, was a wealthy merchant and the owner of a number of business enterprises in Scotland. Owen bought the New Lanark mills from Dale in the summer of 1799 (Podmore, p. 52) and took over their management in January 1800. The details of Owen's financial success in the running of New Lanark are summarised in A. J. Robertson, 'Robert Owen, Cotton Spinner: New Lanark, 1800-1825' in *Robert Owen, Prophet of the Poor, op. cit.,* pp. 145-165.

(5) A. J. Robertson, *loc. cit;* P. Gorb, 'Robert Owen as a Businessman,' *Bulletin of the Business Historical Society,* xxv (1951); S. Pollard, *The Genesis of Modern Management* (London, 1968) *passim.*

(6) 'Between 1815 and 1825 the number of names recorded in the visitors' book was nearly twenty thousand, including the Grand Duke Nicholas of Russia. The village became one of the most visited places in Europe, and for ever after the name of Robert Owen was associated with New Lanark. Many of the visitors recorded their impressions and these accounts were reprinted widely in Owenite and other journals. Few social experiments in the nineteenth century received wider publicity than Owen's work at New Lanark.' J. F. C. Harrison, *Robert Owen . . . op. cit.,* p. 152.

(7) *New View,* p. 27.

(8) *ibid.,* pp. 15-16.

(9) *ibid.,* p. 22.

(10) 'Children are, without exception, passive and wonderfully contrived compounds; which, by an accurate previous and subsequent attention, *founded on a correct knowledge of the subject,* may be formed collectively to have any human character. And although these compounds, like all other works of nature, possess endless varieties, yet they partake of that plastic quality, which, by perseverance under judicious management, may be ultimately moulded into the very image of rational wishes and desires.' *New View,* p. 34.

(11) An important point made by Harold Silver, *The Concept of Popular Education* (London, 1965) in his excellent study of Owen's educational ideas. See especially ch. 2.

(12) *The Life of Robert Owen, op. cit.,* p. 124.

(13) *Address at the City of London Tavern on Thursday, August 21 . . .* in *A Supplementary Appendix to the First Volume of The Life of Robert Owen* Vol. 1A (London, 1858; reprinted Kelley: New York, 1967) p. 115.

(14) *Report to the County of Lanark,* in Vol IA *op. cit.,* pp. 289-290

(15) *ibid.,* p. 285.

(16) E. P. Thompson, *The Making of the English Working Class* (London, 1963) p. 779 ff.

A New View of Society:

OR,

ESSAYS

ON

THE FORMATION

OF

THE HUMAN CHARACTER

Preparatory to the Developement of a Plan for gradually
ameliorating the Condition of

MANKIND.

———

By ROBERT OWEN,

OF NEW LANARK.

———

SECOND EDITION.

———

London:

PRINTED FOR LONGMAN, HURST, REES, ORME, AND BROWN, PATER-
NOSTER ROW; CADELL AND DAVIES, STRAND; J. HATCHARD, PICCA-
DILLY; MURRAY, ALBEMARLE-STREET; CONSTABLE AND CO., AND
OLIPHANT AND CO., EDINBURGH; SMITH AND SONS, AND BRASH
AND REID, GLASGOW; AND SOLD BY ALL THE BOOKSELLERS IN
TOWN AND COUNTRY.

*The profits of this edition will be given to the Association for the relief of the
Manufacturing and Labouring Poor.*

———

1816.

TO

HIS ROYAL HIGHNESS

THE PRINCE REGENT

OF

THE BRITISH EMPIRE.

SIR,

THE following pages are dedicated to Your Royal Highness, not to add to the flattery which has generally been addressed to those of our fellow men who have filled elevated stations; but they claim your protection because they proceed from a Subject of the empire over which you preside, and from one who disregards every inferior consideration in order that he may accomplish the greatest practical good to that empire.

Your Royal Highness, and all who govern the nations of the world, must be conscious that those of high rank, as well as those of inferior situations in life, now experience much misery.

These Essays have been written to show that the origin of that misery may be traced to the ignorance of those who have ruled, and of those who have been governed; to make that ignorance known and evident to all; and to sketch the outlines of a practical Plan, founded altogether on a preventive system, and derived from principles directly opposed to the errors of our forefathers. Should the outlines which have been sketched be formed into a legislative system, and adhered to without deviation, the most important benefits may be anticipated, not only to the subjects of these realms but to the whole human race.

Your Royal Highness and those who direct the polity of other nations have been taught that you have duties to execute; duties, which, with the highest ability and best intentions, cannot, under the prevailing systems of error, be performed.

Hence the dissatisfaction of those for whose

benefit Governments were, or ought to have been, established, and the perplexity and danger of those who govern.

It is concluded with confidence equal to certainty itself, that the principles unfolded in these Essays are competent to develope a practice which, without much apparent change, and without any public disorder, will progressively remove the difficulties of those who in future may rule, and the discontent of those who may be governed.

The language now addressed to Your Royal Highness is the result of a patient observation and extensive experience of human nature; of human nature, not indeed as it is explained in legendary tales of old, but as it now may be read in the living subject—in the words and actions of those among whom we exist.

It is true that many myriads of human beings have been conscientiously deceived; and it may be said, it is most probable that another is now added to the number: it is equally true, however, that similar language has been applied to many, and might have been applied to all who have been the instruments of beneficial improvements.

It may also be said that the principles herein advocated, may nevertheless, like all former theories which have misled mankind, originate in error; in the wild and perverted fancy of a well meaning enthusiast. They have, however, not only been submitted to several of the most intelligent and acute minds of the present day, and who, although urged to the task, have candidly declared they could find no fallacy in the inductions, but they are such, as few, if any, will venture to deny, or scruple to declare that they already admit.

If these principles shall demonstrate themselves to be in unison with every fact which is accessible to us in the present stage of human experience, they will soon prove themselves of a value permanent and substantial, beyond any of the discoveries which have hitherto been made.

Great however as the advantages may prove, the introduction of principles and practices so

*new, unless they are well understood, may cre-
ate a temporary ferment.*

*To prevent the possibility of any such alarm,
the leaders of all the sects and parties in the state
are invited to canvass these principles, and to
endeavour to find error in them, or evil in the
consequences which might follow from their admission into practice.*

*The encouragement of such fair discussion
and examination is all that is now solicited
from Your Royal Highness.*

*Should that discussion and examination prove
them to be erroneous, they will then be, as they
ought to be for the public good, universally con-
demned. On the contrary, should they bear
the test of that investigation to which they are
submitted, and be found, without a single exception, uniformly consistent with all the known
facts of the creation, and consequently true;
then, under the auspices of Your Royal Highness's Administration, mankind will naturally
look for the establishment of such a System in*

the conduct of public affairs as may introduce and perpetuate advantages so eminently important.

That these principles, if true, may give birth to the measures which they immediately recommend; and that Your Royal Highness and the Subjects of these Realms, and the Rulers and Subjects of all other Realms, may in the present age enjoy the advantages of them in practice, is the sincere wish of

Your Royal Highness's faithful Servant,

THE AUTHOR.

ESSAY FIRST.

ON

The Formation of Character.

" Any general character, from the best to the worst, from the most ignorant
to the most enlightened, may be given to any community, even to the world
at large, by the application of proper means; which means are to a great extent at the command and under the controul of those who have influence in
the affairs of men."

TO THE BRITISH PUBLIC.

FRIENDS AND COUNTRYMEN,

I ADDRESS myself to you, because your primary and most essential interests are deeply involved in the subjects treated of in the following Essays.

You will find existing evils described, and remedies proposed; but as those evils proceed from the errors of our forefathers, they seem to call for something like veneration from their successors. You will therefore not attribute them to any of the individuals of the present day; neither will you for your own sakes wish or require them to be prematurely removed. Beneficial changes can only take place by well-digested and well-arranged plans temperately introduced and perseveringly pursued.

It is however an important step gained when the cause of evil is ascertained. The next is to devise a remedy, which shall create the least possible inconvenience. To discover this, and try its efficacy in practice, have been the employments of my life; and having found a remedy which experience proves to be safe in its application, and certain in its effects, I am now anxious that you should all partake of its benefits.

But be satisfied, fully and completely satisfied, that the principles on which the New View of Society is founded are true; that no specious error lurks within them, and that no sinister motive gives rise to their publicity. Let them therefore be investigated to their foundation. Let them be scrutinized with the eye of penetration itself; and let them be compared with every fact which the history of the past or the experience of the present may offer to our view. Let this be done, to give you full confidence, beyond the shadow of doubt or suspicion, in the proceedings which are or may be recommended to your attention. For they will bear this test; and such investigation and comparison will fix them so deeply in your hearts and affections, that never but with life will they be removed from your minds, and from those of your children to the end of time.

Enter therefore fearlessly on the investigation and comparison; startle not at apparent difficulties, but persevere in the spirit and on the principles recommended; you will then speedily overcome those difficulties, your success will be certain, and you will eventually establish the happiness of your fellow-creatures.

That your immediate and united exertions in this cause may be the means of commencing a new system of action, which shall gradually remove the unnecessary evils which afflict the present race of men, is the ardent wish of

THE AUTHOR.

ESSAY FIRST*.

ACCORDING to the last returns under the Population Act, the poor and working classes of Great Britain and Ireland have been found to exceed twelve millions of persons, or nearly three fourths of the population of the British Islands.

The characters of these persons are now permitted to be very generally formed without proper guidance or direction, and, in many cases, under circumstances which directly impel them to a course of extreme vice and misery ; thus rendering them the worst and most dangerous subjects in the empire; while the far greater part of the remainder of the community are educated

---

* The First Essay was written in 1812, and published early in 1813. The Second Essay was written and published at the end of 1813. The Third and Fourth Essays were written, and printed and circulated among the principal political, literary and religious characters in this country and on the continent, as well as among the governments of Europe, America, and British India. They were first printed for sale in July 1816,

upon the most mistaken principles of human nature, such indeed as cannot fail to produce a general conduct throughout society totally unworthy of the character of rational beings.

The first thus unhappily situated are the poor and the uneducated profligate among the working classes, who are now *trained* to *commit* crimes, for the commission of which they are afterwards *punished*.

The second is the remaining mass of the population, who are now *instructed* to *believe*, or at least to acknowledge, that certain principles are *unerringly true*, and to *act* as though they were *grossly false*; thus filling the world with *folly* and *inconsistency*, and making society, throughout all its ramifications, a scene of insincerity and counteraction.

In this state the world has continued to the present time; its evils have been and are continually increasing; they cry aloud for efficient corrective measures, which if we longer delay, general disorder must ensue.

" But," say those who have not deeply investigated the subject, " attempts to apply remedies have been often made, yet all of them have failed. The evil is now of a magnitude not to be controuled ; the torrent is already too strong to be stemmed ; and we can only wait with fear or calm resignation, to see it carry destruction in its course by confounding all distinctions of right and wrong."

Such is the language now held, and such are the general feelings on this most important subject.

These, however, if longer suffered to continue, must lead to the most lamentable consequences. Rather than pursue such a course, the character of legislators would be infinitely raised, if, forgetting the petty and humiliating contentions of sects and parties, they would thoroughly investigate the subject, and endeavour to arrest and overcome these mighty evils.

The chief object of these Essays is to assist and forward investigations of such vital importance to the well-being of this country, and of society in general.

The view of the subject which is about to be given has arisen from extensive experience for upwards of twenty years, during which period its truth and importance have been proved by multiplied experiments. That the writer may not be charged with precipitation or presumption, he has had the principle and its consequences, examined, scrutinized, and fully canvassed by some of the most learned, intelligent, and competent characters of the present day; who on every principle of duty as well as of interest, if they had discovered error in either, would have exposed it;—but who, on the contrary, have fairly acknowledged their incontrovertible truth and practical importance.

Assured, therefore, that his principles are true, he proceeds with confidence, and courts the most ample and free discussion of the subject; courts it for the sake of humanity—for the sake of his fellow creatures—millions of whom experience sufferings, which, were they to be unfolded, would compel those who govern the world to exclaim, " Can these things exist and we have no knowledge of them?" But they do exist— and even the heart-rending statements which were made known to the public during the discussions upon negro - slavery, do not exhibit more afflicting scenes than those which, in various parts of the world, daily arise from the injustice of society towards itself; from the inattention of mankind to the circumstances which incessantly surround them, and from the want of a correct knowledge of human nature in those who govern and controul the affairs of men.

If these circumstances did not exist to an extent almost incredible, it would be unnecessary *now* to contend for a principle regarding Man, which scarcely requires more than to be fairly stated to make it self-evident.

This principle is, that " ANY GENERAL CHA-RACTER, FROM THE BEST TO THE WORST, FROM THE MOST IGNORANT TO THE MOST ENLIGHTENED, MAY BE GIVEN TO ANY COMMUNITY, EVEN TO THE WORLD AT LARGE, BY THE APPLICATION OF PROPER MEANS; WHICH MEANS ARE TO A GREAT EXTENT AT THE COMMAND AND UNDER THE CONTROUL OF THOSE WHO HAVE IN-FLUENCE IN THE AFFAIRS OF MEN."

The principle as now stated is a broad one, and, if it should be found to be true, cannot fail to give a new character to legislative proceedings, and *such* a character as will be most favourable to the well-being of society.

That this principle is true to the utmost limit of the terms, is evident from the experience of all past ages and from every existing fact.

Shall misery, then, most complicated and extensive, be experienced, from the prince to the peasant, throughout all the nations of the world, and shall its cause, and the means of its prevention, be known, and yet these means withheld?

The undertaking is replete with difficulties, which can only be overcome by those who have influence in society; who, by foreseeing its important *practical* benefits, may be induced to contend against those difficulties; and who, when its advantages are clearly seen and strongly felt, will not suffer individual considerations to be put in competition with their attainment. It is true their ease and comfort may be for a time sacrificed to those prejudices; but, if they persevere, the principles on which this knowledge is founded must ultimately universally prevail.

In preparing the way for the introduction of these principles, it cannot now be necessary to enter into the detail of facts to prove that children can be trained to acquire "*any language, sentiments, belief, or any bodily habits and manners, not contrary to human nature.*"

For that this *has* been done, the history of every nation of which we have records abundantly confirms; and that this is, and may be again done, the facts which exist around us and throughout all the countries in the world prove to demonstration.

Possessing then the knowledge of a power so important; which, when understood, is capable of being wielded with the certainty of a law of nature, and which would gradually remove the evils which now chiefly afflict mankind, shall we permit it to remain dormant and useless, and suffer the plagues of society perpetually to exist and increase?

No: the time is *now* arrived when the public mind of this country and the general state of the world call imperatively for the introduction of this all-pervading principle, not only in *theory*, but into *practice*.

Nor can any human power now impede its rapid progress. Silence will not retard its course, and opposition will give increased celerity to its movements. The commencement of the work will, in fact, ensure its accomplishment; henceforth all the irritating, angry passions, arising from ignorance of the true cause of bodily and mental character, will gradually subside, and be replaced by the most frank and conciliating confidence and good-will.

Nor will it be possible hereafter for comparatively a few individuals, unintentionally to occasion the rest of mankind to be surrunded by circumstances which *inevitably* form such characters, as they afterwards deem it a *duty* and a *right to punish even to death ; and that too, while they themselves have been the instruments of forming those characters.* Such proceedings

not only create innumerable evils to the directing few, but essentially retard them and the
great mass of society from attaining the enjoyment of a high degree of positive happiness.
Instead of *punishing* crimes after they have *permitted* the human character to be formed so as
to commit them, they will adopt the only means
which can be adopted to *prevent* the existence
of those crimes; means by which they may be
most easily prevented.

Happily for poor traduced and degraded human nature, the principle for which we now contend will speedily divest it of all the ridiculous
and absurd mystery with which it has been
hitherto enveloped by the ignorance of preceding times: and all the *complicated* and *counteracting* motives for good conduct, which have
been multiplied almost to infinity, will be reduced to *one single principle of action*, which,
by its evident operation and sufficiency, shall
render this intricate system *unnecessary*, and
ultimately supersede it in all parts of the earth.
That principle is THE HAPPINESS OF SELF
CLEARLY UNDERSTOOD AND UNIFORMLY
PRACTISED; WHICH CAN ONLY BE ATTAIN-
ED BY CONDUCT THAT MUST PROMOTE THE
HAPPINESS OF THE COMMUNITY.

For that Power which governs and pervades

the universe has evidently so formed man, that he must progressively pass from a state of ignorance to intelligence, the limits of which it is not for man himself to define ; and in that progress to discover, that his individual happiness can be increased and extended only in proportion as he actively endeavours to increase and extend the happiness of all around him. The principle admits neither of exclusion nor of limitation ; and such appears evidently the state of the public mind, that it will now seize and cherish this principle as the most precious boon which it has yet been allowed to attain. The errors of all opposing motives will appear in their true light, and the ignorance whence they arose will become so glaring, that even the most unenlightened will speedily reject them.

For this state of matters, and for all the gradual changes contemplated, the extraordinary events of the present times have essentially contributed to prepare the way.

Even the late Ruler of France, although *immediately* influenced by the most mistaken principles of ambition, has contributed to this happy result, by shaking to its foundation that mass of superstition and bigotry, which on the continent of Europe had been accumulating for ages, until it had so overpowered and depressed the human intellect, that to attempt improvement without its removal would have been most unavailing. And, in the next place, by carrying the mistaken selfish principles in which mankind have been hitherto educated to the extreme in *practice*, he has rendered their error manifest, and left no doubt of the fallacy of the source whence they originated.

These transactions, in which millions have been immolated, or consigned to poverty and bereft of friends, will be preserved in the records of time, and impress future ages with a just estimation of the principles now about to be introduced into practice; and will thus prove perpetually useful to all succeeding generations.

For the direful effects of Napoleon's government have created the most deep-rooted disgust at notions which could produce a belief that such conduct was glorious, or calculated to increase the happiness of even the individual by whom it was pursued.

And the late discoveries, and proceedings of the Rev. Dr. Bell and Mr. Joseph Lancaster, have also been preparing the way in a manner the most opposite, but yet not less effectual, by directing the public attention to the beneficial effects, on the young and unresisting mind, of even the limited education which their systems embrace.

They have already effected enough to prove that all which is now in contemplation respecting the training of youth may be accomplished without fear of disappointment. And by so doing, as the consequences of their improvements cannot be confined within the British Isles, they will for ever be ranked among the most important benefactors of the human race. But henceforward to contend for any new *exclusive* system will be in vain : the public mind is already too well informed, and has too far passed the possibility of retrogression, much longer to permit the continuance of any such evil.

For it is now obvious that such a system must be destructive of the happiness of the excluded, by their seeing others enjoy what they are not permitted to possess ; and also that it tends, by creating opposition from the justly injured feelings of the excluded, in proportion to the extent of the exclusion, to diminish the happiness even of the privileged : the former therefore can have no rational motive for its continuance. If however, owing to the irrational principles by which the world has been hitherto governed, in-i viduals, or sects, or parties, shall yet by their plans of exclusion attempt to retard the amelioration of society, and prevent the introduction into PRACTICE of that truly just spirit which knows *no* exclusion, such facts shall yet be brought forward as cannot fail to render all their efforts vain. It will therefore be the essence of wisdom in the privileged classes to cooperate sincerely and cordially with those who desire not to touch one iota of the supposed advantages which they *now* possess; and whose first and last wish is to increase the particular happiness of those classes as well as the general happiness of society. A very little reflection on the part of the privileged will insure this line of conduct; whence, without domestic revolution —without war and bloodshed—nay without prematurely disturbing any thing which exists, the world will be prepared to receive principles which are alone calculated to build up a system of happiness, and to destroy those irritable feelings which have so long afflicted society,— solely because society has hitherto been ignorant of the true means by which the most useful and valuable character may be formed.

This ignorance being removed, experience will soon teach us how to form character, individually and generally, so as to give the greatest sum of happiness to the individual, and to mankind.

These principles require only to be known in order to establish themselves: the outline of our future proceedings then becomes clear and defined, nor will they permit us henceforth to wander from the right path. They direct that the governing powers of all countries should establish rational plans for the education and general formation of the characters of their subjects.——*These plans must be devised to train children from their earliest infancy in good habits of every description (which will of course prevent them from acquiring those of falsehood and deception). They must afterwards be rationally educated, and their labour be usefully directed. Such habits and education will impress them with an active and ardent desire to promote the happiness of every individual, and that without the shadow of exception for sect, or party, or country, or climate. They will also insure, with the fewest possible exceptions, health, strength, and vigour of body; for the happiness of man can be erected only on the foundations of health of body and peace of mind.*

And that health of body and peace of mind may be preserved sound and entire, through youth and manhood, to old age, it becomes *equally* necessary that the irresistible propensities which form part of his nature, and which now produce the endless and ever multiplying evils with which humanity is afflicted, should be so directed as to *increase* and not to *counteract* his happiness.

The knowledge however thus introduced will make it evident to the understanding, that by far the greater part of the misery with which man is encircled *may* be easily dissipated and removed ; and that with mathematical precision he *may be* surrounded with those circumstances which must gradually increase his happiness.

Hereafter, when the public at large shall be satisfied that these principles *can* and *will* withstand the ordeal through which they must inevitably pass ; when they shall prove themselves true to the clear comprehension and certain conviction of the unenlightened as well as the learned ; and when by the irresistible power of truth, detached from falsehood, they shall establish themselves in the mind, no more to be removed but by the entire annihilation of the human intellects ; then the consequent practice which they direct shall be explained, and rendered easy of adoption.

In the mean time, let no one anticipate evil,

even in the slightest degree, from these principles; they are, not innoxious only, but preg-
nant with consequences to be wished and desired beyond all others by *every* individual in
society.

Some of the best intentioned among the various classes in society may still say, " All this
is *very delightful and very beautiful* in *theory*,
but *visionaries* alone can expect to see it *re-
alized*." To this remark only one reply *can* or
ought to be made; that *these principles have
been carried most successfully into practice**.
The present Essays therefore are not brought
forward as mere matter of speculation, to amuse
the idle visionary who *thinks* in his closet and
never *acts* in the world; but to create universal
activity, pervade society with a knowledge of
its true interests, and direct the public mind to
the most important object to which it can be
directed; to a national proceeding for rationally
forming the characters of that immense mass of
population which is now allowed to be so formed
as to fill the world with crimes. Shall questions

---

* The beneficial effects of this practice have been experienced for many years among a population of between two
and three thousand at New Lanark in Scotland.

of merely local and temporary interest, whose ultimate results are calculated only to withdraw pecuniary profits from one set of individuals and give them to others, engage day after day the attention of politicians and ministers; call forth petitions and delegates from the widely spread agricultural and commercial interests of the empire;—and shall the well-being of millions of the poor, half-naked, half-famished, untaught and untrained, hourly increasing to a most alarming extent in these islands, not call forth *one* petition, *one* delegate, or *one* rational effective legislative measure? No! for such has been our education, that we hesitate not to devote years and expend millions in the *detection* and *punishment* of crimes, and in the attainment of objects whose ultimate results are in comparison with this insignificancy itself; and yet we have not moved one step in the true path to *prevent* crimes, and to diminish the innumerable evils with which mankind are now afflicted. Are these false principles of conduct in those who govern the world to influence mankind permanently,—and if not, *how* and *when* is the change to commence? These important considerations shall form the subject of the next essay.

SECOND ESSAY.

THE PRINCIPLES OF THE FORMER ESSAY

CONTINUED AND APPLIED IN PART TO PRACTICE.

———

" It is not unreasonable to hope that *hostility may cease*, even where *perfect agreement cannot be established.* If we cannot *reconcile all opinions,* let us endeavour *to unite all hearts.*" Mr. Vansittart's Letter to the Rev. Dr. Herbert Marsh.

———

ESSAY SECOND.

GENERAL principles only were developed in the First Essay. In this an attempt will be made to show the advantages which may be derived from the adoption of those principles into practice, and to explain the mode by which the practice may without inconvenience be generally introduced.

Some of the most important benefits to be derived from the introduction of those principles into practice are, that they will create the most cogent reasons to induce each man " to have charity for *all* men." No feeling short of this can indeed find place in any mind which has been taught clearly to understand, that children in all parts of the earth have been, are, and everlastingly will be impressed with habits and sentiments similar to those of their parents and instructors; modified, however, by the circumstances in which they have been, are, or may be placed, and by the peculiar original organization of each individual. Yet not one of these causes of character is at the command, or in any manner under the control, of infants, who (whatever absurdity we may have been taught to the contrary) cannot possibly be accountable for the sentiments and manners which may be given to them. And here lies the fundamental error of society, and from hence have proceeded, and do proceed, most of the miseries of mankind.

Children are, without exception, passive and wonderfully contrived compounds; which, by an accurate previous and subsequent attention, *founded on a correct knowledge of the subject*, may be formed collectively to have any human character. And although these compounds, like all the other works of nature, possess endless varieties, yet they partake of that plastic quality, which, by perseverance under judicious management, may be ultimately moulded into the very image of rational wishes and desires.

In the next place, these principles cannot fail to create feelings, which without force, or the production of any counteracting motive, will irresistibly lead those who possess them to make due allowance for the difference of sentiments and manners, not only among their friends and countrymen, but also among the inhabitants of every region of the earth, even including their enemies. With this insight into the formation of character, there is no conceivable foundation for private displeasure or public enmity. Say, if it be within the sphere of possibility that children can be trained to attain *that* knowledge, and at the same time to acquire feelings of enmity towards a single human creature? The child who from infancy has been rationally instructed in these principles, will readily discover and trace *whence* the opinions and habits of his associates have arisen, and *why* they possess them. At the same age he will have acquired reasons sufficient to exhibit to him forcibly the irrationality of being angry with an individual for possessing qualities which, as a passive being during the formation of those qualities, he had not the means of preventing. Such are the impressions these principles will make on the mind of every child so taught; and instead of generating anger or displeasure, they will produce commiseration and pity for those individuals who possess either habits or sentiments which appear to him to be destructive of their own comfort, pleasure, or happiness; and will produce on his part a desire to remove those causes of distress, that his own feelings of commiseration and pity may be also removed. The pleasure which he cannot avoid experiencing by this mode of conduct will likewise stimulate him to the most active endeavours to withdraw those circumstances which surround any part of mankind with causes of misery, and to replace them with others which have a tendency to increase happiness. He will then also strongly entertain the desire to " do good to *all* men," and even to those who think themselves his enemies.

Thus *shortly*, *directly*, and *certainly* may mankind be taught the *essence*, and to attain the *ultimate object*, of all former *moral* and *religious* instruction.

These essays, however, are intended to explain that which is *true*, and not to attack that which is *false*. For to explain that which is true may permanently improve, without creating even temporary evil; whereas to attack that which is false, is often productive of very fatal consequences. The former convinces the judgement, when the mind possesses full and deliberative powers of judging; the latter instantly arouses irritation, and renders the judgement unfit for its office, and useless. But why should we *ever* irritate? Do not these principles make it so obvious as to place it beyond any doubt, that even the present irrational ideas and practices prevalent throughout the world, are not to be charged as either a fault or culpable error of the existing generation? The immediate cause of them was the partial ignorance of our forefathers, who, although they acquired some vague disjointed knowledge of the principles on which character is formed, could not discover the connected chain of those principles, and consequently knew not how to apply them to practice. They taught their children that which they had themselves been taught, that which they had acquired; and in so doing they acted like their forefathers; who retained the established customs of former generations until better and superior were discovered and made evident to them.

The present race of men have also instructed their children as they had been previously instructed, and are equally unblameable for any defects which their systems contain. And however erroneous or injurious that instruction and those systems may now be proved to be, the principles on which these essays are founded will be misunderstood, and their spirit will be wholly misconceived, if either irritation, or the slightest degree of ill will, shall be generated against those who even tenaciously adhere to the worst parts of that instruction, and support the most pernicious of those systems. For such individuals, sects, or parties have been trained from infancy to consider it their duty and interest so to act, and in so acting they merely continue the customs of their predecessors. Let truth unaccompanied with error be placed before them ; give them time to examine it, and see that it is in unison with all previously ascertained truths, and conviction and acknowledgement of it will follow of course. It is weakness itself to require assent *before* conviction, and *afterwards* it will not be withheld. To endeavour to force conclusions, without making the subject clear to the understanding, is most unjustifiable and irrational, and must prove useless or injurious to the mental faculties. In the spirit thus described we therefore proceed in the investigation of the subject.

The facts which by the invention of printing have gradually accumulated, now show the errors of the systems of our forefathers so distinctly, that they must be, when pointed out, evident to all classes of the community, and render it absolutely necessary that new legislative measures be immediately adopted, to prevent the confusion which must arise from even the most ignorant being competent to detect the absurdity and glaring injustice of many of those laws by which they are now governed.

Such are those laws which enact punishments for a very great variety of actions designated crimes; while those from whom such actions proceed, are regularly trained to acquire no other knowledge than that which compels them to conclude, that those actions are the best they could perform.

How much longer shall we continue to allow generation after generation to be taught crime from their infancy, and, when so taught, hunt them like beasts of the forests, until they are entangled beyond escape in the toils and nets of the law? when, if the circumstances of those poor unpitied sufferers had been reversed with those who are even surrounded with the pomp and dignity of justice, these latter would have been at the bar of the culprit, and the former would have been in the judgement seat.

Had the present Judges of these realms been born and educated among the poor and profligate of St. Giles's, or some similar situation, is it not certain, inasmuch as they possess native energies and abilities, that ere this they would have been at the head of their *then* profession, and, in consequence of that superiority and pro-

ficiency, would have already suffered imprison-
ment, transportation, or death? Can we for a
moment hesitate to decide, that, if some of those
men whom the laws, dispensed by the present
Judges, have doomed to suffer capital punishments, had been born, trained, and circumstanced as these Judges were born, trained, and
circumstanced; that some of those who had so
suffered, would have been the identical individuals who would have passed the same awful
sentences on the present highly esteemed dignitaries of the law?

If we open our eys and attentively notice
events, we shall observe these facts to multiply
before us. Is the evil then of so small magnitude as to be totally disregarded and passed by as
the ordinary occurrences of the day, and as not
deserving of one reflection? And shall we be
longer told, " that the convenient time to attend to inquiries of this nature is not yet come;
that other matters of far weightier import engage our attention, and it must remain over till
a season of more leisure?"

To those who may be inclined to think and
speak thus, I would say, " Let feelings of humanity or strict justice induce you to devote a
few hours to visit some of the public prisons of

the metropolis, and patiently inquire, with kind commiserating solicitude, of their various inhabitants, the events of their lives, and the lives of their connections. They will tales unfold that *must* arrest attention, that will disclose *sufferings, misery,* and *injustice,* upon which, for obvious reasons, I will not now dwell, but which, previously, I am persuaded, you could not suppose it possible to exist in any civilized state, far less that they should be permitted for centuries to increase around the very fountain of British jurisprudence. The true cause however of this conduct, so contrary to the general humanity of the natives of these Islands, is, that a practicable remedy for the evil, on clearly defined and sound principles, had not yet been suggested. But the principles developed in this "New View of Society" *will point out a remedy which is almost simplicity itself, possessing no more practical difficulties than many of the common employments of life; and such as are readily overcome by men of very ordinary practical talents.*

That such a remedy is easily practicable, may be collected from the account of the following very partial experiment.

In the year 1784 the late Mr. Dale of Glasgow founded a manufactory for spinning of cotton near the falls of the Clyde, in the county of Lanark in Scotland; and about that period cotton mills were first introduced into the northern part of the kingdom.

It was the power which could be obtained from the falls of water which induced Mr. Dale to erect his mills in this situation, for in other respects it was not well chosen; the country around was uncultivated; the inhabitants were poor, and few in number; and the roads in the neighbourhood were so bad, that the Falls now so celebrated were then unknown to strangers.

It was therefore necessary to collect a new population to supply the infant establishment with labourers. This however was no light task; for all the regularly trained Scotch peasantry disdained the idea of working early and late, day after day, within cotton mills. Two modes then only remained of obtaining these labourers: the one, to procure children from the various public charities of the country; and the other, to induce families to settle around the works.

To accommodate the first, a large house was erected, which ultimately contained about five hundred children, who were procured chiefly from workhouses and charities in Edinburgh. These children were to be fed, clothed, and educated; and these duties Mr. Dale performed with the unwearied benevolence which it is well known he possessed.

To obtain the second, a village was built, and the houses were let at a low rent to such families as could be induced to accept employment in the mills: but such was the general dislike to that occupation at the time, that, with a few exceptions, only persons destitute of friends, employment, and character, were found willing to try the experiment; and of these a sufficient number to supply a constant increase of the manufactory could not be obtained. It was therefore deemed a favour on the part even of such individuals to reside at the village, and when taught the business they grew so valuable to the establishment, that they became agents not to be governed contrary to their own inclinations.

Mr. Dale's principal avocations were at a distance from the works, which he seldom visited more than once for a few hours in three or four months: he was therefore under the necessity of committing the management of the establishment to various servants with more or less power.

Those who have a practical knowledge of mankind will readily anticipate the character which a population so collected and constituted would acquire; it is therefore scarcely necessary to state, that the community by degrees was formed under these circumstances into a very wretched society; every man did that which was right in his own eyes, and vice and immorality prevailed to a monstrous extent. The population lived in idleness, in poverty, in almost every kind of crime; consequently in debt, out of health, and in misery. Yet to make matters still worse,—although the cause proceeded from the best possible motive, a conscientious adherence to principle,—the whole was under a strong sectarian influence, which gave a marked and decided preference to one set of religious opinions over all others, and the professors of the favoured opinions were the privileged of the community.

The boarding-house containing the children presented a very different scene. The benevolent proprietor spared no expense to give comfort to the poor children. The rooms provided for them were spacious, always clean, and well ventilated; the food was abundant, and of the best quality; the clothes were neat and useful; a surgeon was kept in constant pay to direct how to prevent or to cure disease; and the best instructors which the country afforded were appointed to teach such branches of education as were deemed likely to be useful to children in their situation. Kind and well disposed persons were appointed to superintend all their proceedings. Nothing, in short, at first sight seemed wanting to render it a most complete charity.

But to defray the expense of these well devised arrangements, and support the establishment generally, it was absolutely necessary that the children should be employed within the mills from six o'clock in the morning till seven in the evening, summer and winter; and after these hours their education commenced. The directors of the public charities, from mistaken œconomy, would not consent to send the children under their care to cotton mills, unless the children were received by the proprietors at the ages of six, seven, and eight. And Mr. Dale was under the necessity of accepting them at those ages, or of stopping the manufactory which he had commenced.

It is not to be supposed that children so young could remain, with the interval of meals only, from six in the morning until seven in the evening, in constant employment on their feet within cotton mills, and afterwards acquire much proficiency in education. And so it proved; for many of them became dwarfs in body and mind, and some of them were deformed. Their labour through the day, and their education at night, became so irksome, that numbers of them continually ran away, and almost all looked forward with impatience and anxiety to the expiration of their apprenticeship of seven, eight, and nine years; which generally expired when they were from thirteen to fifteen years old. At this period of life, unaccustomed to provide for themselves, and unacquainted with the world, they usually went to Edinburgh or Glasgow, where boys and girls were soon assailed by the innumerable temptations which all large towns present; and to which many of them fell sacrifices.

Thus Mr. Dale's arrangements and kind solicitude for the comfort and happiness of these children were rendered in their ultimate effect almost nugatory. They were hired by him, and sent to be employed, and without their labour he could not support them; but, while under his care, he did all that any individual, circumstanced as he was, could do for his fellow-creatures. The error proceeded from the children being sent from the workhouses at an age much too young for employment; they ought to have been detained four years longer, and educated; and then some of the evils which followed would have been prevented.

If such be a true picture, not overcharged, of parish apprentices to our manufacturing system, under the best and most humane regulations, in what colours must it be exhibited under the worst?

Mr. Dale was advancing in years; he had no son to succeed him; and finding the consequences just described to be the result of all his strenuous exertions for the improvement and happiness of his fellow-creatures, it is not surprising that he became disposed to retire from the cares of the establishment. He accordingly sold it to some English merchants and manufacturers; one of whom, under the circumstances just narrated, undertook the management of the concern, and fixed his residence in the midst of the population. This individual had been previously in the management of large establishments, employing a number of work-people in the neighbourhood of Manchester; and in every case, by the steady application of certain general principles, he succeeded in reforming the habits of those under his care, and who always among their associates in similar employment appeared conspicuous for their good conduct. With this previous success in remodelling English character, but ignorant of the local ideas, manners, and customs of those now committed to his management, the stranger commenced his task.

At that period the lower classes in Scotland, like those of other countries, had strong prejudices against strangers having any authority over them, and particularly against the English; few of whom had then settled in Scotland, and not one in the neighbourhood of the scenes under description. It is also well known that even the Scotch peasantry and working classes possess the habit of making observations and reasoning thereon with great acuteness; and in the present case, those employed naturally concluded that the new purchasers intended merely to make the utmost profit by the establishment, from the abuses of which many of themselves were then deriving support. The persons employed at these works were therefore strongly prejudiced against the new director of the establishment; prejudiced, because he was a stranger and from England; because he succeeded Mr. Dale, under whose proprietorship they acted almost as they liked; because his religious creed was not theirs; and because they concluded that the works would be governed by new laws and regulations, calculated to squeeze, as they often termed it, the greatest sum of gain out of their labour.

In consequence, from the day he arrived among them, every means which ingenuity could devise was set to work to counteract the plan which he attempted to introduce; and for two years it was a regular attack and defence of prejudices and mal-practices between the manager and population of the place; without the former being able to make much progress, or convince the latter of the sincerity of his good intentions for their welfare. He however did not lose his patience, his temper, or his confidence in the certain success of the principles on which he founded his conduct. These principles ultimately prevailed: the population could not continue to resist a firm well-directed kindness administering justice to all. They therefore slowly and cautiously began to give him some portion of their confidence; and, as this increased, he was enabled more and more to develope his plans for their amelioration. It may with truth be said, that at this period they possessed almost all the vices and very few of the virtues of a social com-

munity. Theft and the receipt of stolen goods
was their trade, idleness and drunkenness their
habit, falsehood and deception their garb, dissentions civil and religious their daily practice:
they united only in a zealous systematic opposition to their employers.

Here, then, was a fair field on which to try
the efficacy in practice of principles supposed
capable of altering any characters. The manager formed his plans accordingly: he spent
some time in finding out the full extent of the
evil against which he had to contend, and in
tracing the true causes which had produced, and
were continuing, those effects. He found that
all was distrust, disorder, and disunion; and he
wished to introduce confidence, regularity, and
harmony: he therefore began to bring forward
his various expedients to withdraw the unfavourable circumstances by which they had been
hitherto surrounded, and replace them by others
calculated to produce a more happy result. He
soon discovered that theft was extended through
almost all the ramifications of the community,
and the receipt of stolen goods through all the
country around. To remedy this evil, not one
legal punishment was inflicted, not one individual imprisoned, even for an hour: but checks

and other regulations of prevention were introduced ; a short plain explanation of the immediate benefits they would derive from a different conduct was inculcated by those instructed for the purpose, who had the best powers of reasoning among themselves. They were at the same time instructed how to direct their industry in legal and useful occupations ; by which, without danger or disgrace, they could really earn more than they had previously obtained by dishonest practices.—Thus, the difficulty of committing the crime was increased, the detection afterwards rendered more easy, the habit of honest industry formed, and the pleasure of good conduct experienced.

Drunkenness was attacked in the same manner : it was discountenanced on every occasion by those who had charge of any department : its destructive and pernicious effects were frequently stated by his own more prudent comrades, at the proper moment, when the individual was soberly suffering from the effects of his previous excess : pot- and public-houses were gradually removed from the immediate vicinity of their dwellings: the health and comfort of temperance were made familiar to them : by degrees drunkenness disappeared, and many who were habitual bacchanalians are now conspicuous for undeviating sobriety.

Falsehood and deception met with a similar fate; they were held in disgrace, their practical evils were shortly explained; and every countenance was given to truth and open conduct. The pleasure and substantial advantages derived from the latter, soon overcame the impolicy, error, and consequent misery which the former mode of acting had created.

Dissentions and quarrels were undermined by analogous expedients. When they could not be readily adjusted between the parties themselves, they were stated to the manager; and as in such cases both disputants were usually more or less in the wrong, that wrong was in as few words as possible explained, forgiveness and friendship recommended, and one simple and easily remembered precept inculcated, as the most valuable rule for their whole conduct, and the advantages of which they would experience every moment of their lives:—viz. "That in future they should endeavour to use the same active exertions to make each other happy and comfortable, as they had hitherto done to make each other miserable; and, by carrying this short memorandum in their mind, and applying it on all occasions, they would soon render that place a paradise, which, from the most mistaken principles of action, they now made the abode of misery."—The experiment was tried, the parties enjoyed the gratification of this new mode of conduct; references rapidly subsided, and now serious differences are scarcely known.

Considerable jealousies also existed on account of one religious sect possessing a decided preference over the others. This was corrected by discontinuing that preference, and giving an uniform encouragement to those who conducted themselves well, among all the various religious persuasions; by recommending the same consideration to be shown to the conscientious opinions of each sect, on the ground that all must believe the particular doctrines which they had been taught, and consequently all were in that respect upon an equal footing; nor was it possible yet to say which was right, or which wrong. It was likewise inculcated, that all should attend to the essence of religion, and not act as the world was now taught and trained to do: that is, to overlook the substance and essence of religion, and devote their talents, time, and money, to that which is far worse than its shadow, sectarianism; another term for something very in-

jurious to society, and very absurd, which one
or other well meaning enthusiast has added to
true religion; which, without these defects,
would soon form those characters which every
wise and good man is anxious to see.

Such statements and conduct arrested sectarian animosity and ignorant intolerance; each
retains full liberty of conscience, and in consequence each partakes of the sincere friendship
of many sects instead of one. They act with
cordiality together in the same departments and
pursuits, and associate as though the whole community were not of different sectarian persuasions: and not one evil ensues.

The same principles were applied to correct
the irregular intercourse of the sexes;—such
conduct was discountenanced and held in disgrace; fines were levied upon both parties for
the use of the support fund * of the community.
But because they had once unfortunately of-
fended against the established laws and customs
of society, they were not forced to become vicious, abandoned, and miserable. The door

---

* This fund arose from each individual contributing one
sixtieth part of their wages, which, under their own management, was applied to support the sick, the injured by accident,
and the aged.

was left open for them to return to the comforts of kind friends and respected acquaintance; and, beyond any previous expectation, the evil became greatly diminished.

The system of receiving apprentices from public charities was abolished; permanent settlers with large families were encouraged, and comfortable houses were built for their accommodation.

The practice of employing children in the mills, of six, seven, and eight years of age, was discontinued, and their parents advised to allow them to acquire health and education until they were ten years old *.

The children were taught reading, writing, and arithmetic, during five years, that is, from five to ten, in the village school, without ex-

---

* It may be remarked, that even this age is too early to keep them at constant employment in manufactories from six in the morning to seven in the evening. Far better would it be for the children, their parents, and for society, that the first should not commence employment until they attain the age of twelve, when their education might be finished, and their bodies would be more competent to undergo the fatigue and exertions required of them. When parents can be trained to afford this additional time to their children without inconvenience, they will, of course, adopt the practice now recommended.

pense to their parents. All the modern improvements in education have been adopted, or are in process of adoption *. They may therefore be taught and well trained before they engage in any regular employment. Another important consideration is, that all their instruction is rendered a pleasure and delight to them; they are much more anxious for the hour of school time to arrive than to end: they therefore make a rapid progress; and it may be safely asserted, that if they shall not be trained to form such characters as may be the most desired, the fault will not proceed from the children; the cause will be in the want of a true knowledge of human nature in those who have the management of them and their parents.

During the period that these changes were going forward, attention was given to the domestic arrangements of the community. Their houses were rendered more comfortable, their streets were improved, the best provisions were purchased, and sold to them at low rates, yet

---

* To avoid the inconveniences which must ever arise from the introduction of a particular creed into a school, the children are taught to read in such books as inculcate those precepts of the Christian religion which are common to all denominations.

covering the original expense; and under such regulations as taught them how to proportion their expenditure to their income. Fuel and clothes were obtained for them in the same manner; and no advantage was ever attempted to be taken of them, or means used to deceive them.

In consequence, their animosity and opposition to the stranger subsided, their full confidence was obtained, and they became satisfied that no evil was intended them: they were convinced that a real desire existed to increase their happiness, upon those grounds alone on which it could be permanently increased. All difficulties in the way of future improvement vanished. They were taught to be rational, and they acted rationally; thus both parties experienced the incalculable advantages of the system which had been adopted. Those employed became industrious, temperate, healthy; faithful to their employers, and kind to each other; while the proprietors were deriving services from their attachment, almost without inspection, far beyond those which could be obtained by any other means than those of mutual confidence and kindness. Such was the effect of these principles on the adults; on those whose previous habits had been as ill formed as habits could be; and certainly the application of the principles to practice was made under the most unfavourable circumstances *.

I have thus given a detailed account of this experiment, although a partial application of the principles is of far less importance than a clear and accurate account of the principles themselves, in order that they may be so well understood as to be easily rendered applicable to practice in any community, and under any circumstances. Without this, particular facts may indeed amuse or astonish, but they would not contain that substantial value which the principles will be found to possess. But if the relation of the narrative shall forward this object, the experiment cannot fail to prove the certain means of renovating the moral and religious principles of the world; by showing whence arise the various opinions, manners, vices, and

---

* It may be supposed that this community was separated from other society; but the supposition would be erroneous, for it had daily and hourly communicatiou with a population exceeding itself. The royal borough of Lanark is only one mile distant from the works; many individuals come daily from the former to be employed at the latter; and a general intercourse is constantly maintained between the old and new towns.

virtues of mankind; and how the best or the worst of them may, with mathematical precision, be taught to the rising generations.

Let it not, therefore, be longer said that evil or injurious actions cannot be prevented; or that the most rational habits in the rising generation cannot be universally formed. In those characters which now exhibit crime, the fault is obviously not in the individual, but the defect proceeds from the system in which the individual has been trained. Withdraw those circumstances which ténd to create crime in the human character, and crime will not be created. Replace them with such as are calculated to form habits of order, regularity, temperance, industry, and these qualities will be formed. Adopt measures of fair equity and justice, and you will readily acquire the full and complete confidence of the lower orders: proceed systematically on principles of undeviating persevering kindness, yet retaining and using, with the least possible severity, the means of restraining crime from immediately injuring society; and by degrees, even the crimes now existing in the adults will also gradually disappear; for the worst formed disposition, short of incurable insanity, will not long resist a firm, determined, well directed, persevering kindness. Such a proceeding, when-ever practised, will be found the most powerful and effective corrector of crime, and of all inju-rious and improper habits.

The experiment narrated shows that this is not hypothesis and theory. The principles may be with confidence stated to be universal, and applicable to all times, persons, and circum-stances. And the most obvious application of them would be, to adopt rational means to re-move the temptation to commit crimes, and increase the difficulties of committing them; while, at the same time, a proper direction should be given to the active powers of the in-dividual, and a due share provided of uninju-rious amusements and recreation. Care must be also taken to remove the causes of jealousy, dissentions, and irritation; to introduce senti-ments calculated to create union and confidence among all the members of the community; and the whole should be directed by a persevering kindness, sufficiently evident to prove that a sincere desire exists to increase, and not to di-minish, happiness.

These principles, applied to the community at New Lanark, at first under many of the most discouraging circumstances, but persevered in

for sixteen years, effected a complete change in
the general character of the village, containing
upwards of two thousand inhabitants, and into
which, also, there was a constant influx of new
comers.—But as the promulgation of new mi-
racles is not for present times, it is not pre-
tended that under such circumstances one and
all are become wise and good; or, that they are
free from error: but it may be truly stated,
that they now constitute a very improved society, that their worst habits are gone, and that
their minor ones will soon disappear under a continuance of the application of the same principles; that during the period mentioned, scarcely
a legal punishment has been inflicted, or an application been made for parish funds by any individual among them. Drunkenness is not seen
in their streets, and the children are taught and
trained in the institution for forming their character without any punishment. The community exhibits the general appearance of industry,
temperance, comfort, health, and happiness.—
These are and ever will be the sure and certain
effects of the adoption of the principles explained; and these principles, applied with judgement, will effectually reform the most vicious

community existing, and train the younger part of it to any character which may be desired; and that, too, much more easily on an extended than on a limited scale.—To apply these principles, however, successfully to practice, both a comprehensive and a minute view must be taken of the existing state of the society on which they are intended to operate. The causes of the most prevalent evils must be accurately traced, and those means which appear the most easy and simple should be immediately applied to remove them.

In this progress the smallest alteration, adequate to produce any good effect, should be made at one time; indeed, if possible, the change should be so gradual as to be almost imperceptible, yet always making a permanent advance in the desired improvements. By this procedure the most rapid practical progress will be obtained, because the inclination to resistance will be removed, and time will be given for reason to weaken the force of long established injurious prejudices. The removal of the first evil will prepare the way for the removal of the second; and this facility will increase, not in an arithmetical, but in a geometrical proportion;

until the directors of the system will themselves be gratified beyond expression with the beneficial magnitude of their own proceedings.

Nor while these principles shall be acted upon can there be any retrogression in this good work; for the permanence of the amelioration will be equal to its extent.

What then remains to prevent such a system from being immediately adopted into national practice? Nothing, surely, but a general distribution of the knowledge of the practice. For, with the certain means of preventing crimes, can it be supposed that British legislators, as soon as these means shall be made evident, will longer withhold them from their fellow subjects? No: I am persuaded that neither prince, ministers, parliament, nor any party in church or state, will avow inclination to act on principles of such flagrant injustice. Have they not on many occasions evinced a sincere and ardent desire to ameliorate the condition of the subjects of the empire, when practicable means of amelioration were explained to them, which could be adopted without risking the safety of the state? They have, it is true, refused one measure called a reform, and most wise have they been in persevering in that refusal. But the advocates for that measure, well-intentioned and patriotic as many of them are, cannot show any good practical effects to be derived from it in the present state of ignorance in which the mass of the British population has been hitherto allowed to be trained. On the contrary, no rational being can attentively observe the scenes exhibited during every general election, and wish for those scenes to be extended. That, indeed, would be to wish any thing but a reform of the manners, habits and principles of our abused and deluded fellow subjects. Nor is it easy to say which most deserve our pity and commiseration; those who, with some pretensions to knowledge, adopt every low art to deceive,—to engender the most pernicious habits,—nay, to foster crime which they afterwards enact laws to punish,—or those whose welfare and substantial comforts are sacrificed to such proceedings.

Away then with this abuse of terms! It would not, and while the present circumstances continue, it could not be reform ; but, if now adopted, it would soon terminate in anarchy and confusion.

For some time to come there can be but one practicable, and therefore one rational reform, which without danger can be attempted in these realms; a reform in which all men and all parties may join—that is, a reform in the training and in the management of the poor, the ignorant, the untaught and untrained, or ill taught and ill trained, among the whole mass of British population; and a plain, simple, practicable plan, which would not contain the least danger to any individual, or to any part of society, may be devised for that purpose.

That plan is a national, well digested, unexclusive system for the formation of character, and general amelioration of the lower orders. On the experience of a life devoted to the subject I hesitate not to say, that the members of any community may by degrees be trained to live *without idleness, without poverty, without crime, and without punishment*; for each of these is the effect of error in the various systems prevalent throughout the world. *They are all the necessary consequences of ignorance.*

Train any population rationally, and they will be rational. Furnish honest and useful employments to those so trained, and such employments they will greatly prefer to dishonest or injurious occupations. It is beyond all calculation the interest of every government to provide that training and that employment : and to provide both is easily practicable.

The first, as before stated, is to be obtained by a national system for the formation of character; the second, by governments preparing a reserve of employment for the surplus working classes, when the general demand for labour throughout the country is not equal to the full occupation of the whole : that employment to be on useful national objects, from which the public may derive advantage equal to the expense which those works may require.

The national plan for the formation of character should *include* all the modern improvements of education, without regard to the system of any one individual ; and should not *exclude* the child of any one subject in the empire. Any thing short of this would be an act of intolerance and injustice to the excluded, and of injury to society, so glaring and manifest, that I shall be deceived in the character of my countrymen, if any of those who have influence in church or state should now be found willing to attempt it. Is it not indeed strikingly evident even to common observers, that any further effort to enforce religious exclusion would involve the certain and speedy destruction of the present church establishment, and would even endanger our civil institutions?

It may be said, however, that ministers and parliament have many other important subjects under discussion. This is evidently true; but will they not have high national concerns always to engage their attention? And can any question be brought forward of deeper interest to the community than that which affects the formation of character and the well-being of every individual within the empire? a question too which, when understood, will be found to offer the means of amelioration to the revenues of these kingdoms, far beyond any practical plan now likely to be devised. Yet, important as are considerations of revenue, they must appear secondary when put in competition with the lives, liberty, and comfort of our fellow subjects; which are now hourly sacrificed for want of an *effective legislative measure to prevent crime.* And is an act of such vital importance to the well-being of all to be longer delayed? *Shall yet another year pass in which crime shall be forced on the infant, who in ten, twenty, or thirty years hence shall suffer* DEATH *for being taught that crime?* Surely it is impossible. Should it be so delayed, *the individuals of the present par-*

liament, the legislators of this day, ought in strict and impartial justice to be amenable to the laws, for not adopting the means in their power to prevent the crime; rather than the poor, untrained, and unprotected culprit, whose previous years, if he had language to describe them, would exhibit a life of unceasing wretchedness, arising *solely* from the errors of society.

Much might be added on these momentous subjects, even to make them evident to the capacities of children: but for obvious reasons the outlines are merely sketched; and it is hoped these outlines will be sufficient to induce the well-disposed of all parties cordially to unite in this vital measure for the preservation of every thing dear to society.

In the next Essay an account will be given of the plans which are in progress at New Lanark for the further comfort and improvement of its inhabitants; and a general *practical* system be described, by which the same advantages may be gradually introduced among the poor and working classes throughout the united kingdom.

ESSAY THIRD.

THE PRINCIPLES OF THE FORMER ESSAYS

APPLIED TO

A Particular Situation.

Truth must ultimately prevail over Error.

AN ADDRESS

To the Superintendants of Manufactories, and to those Individuals generally, who, by giving Employment to an aggregated Population, may easily adopt the Means to form the Sentiments and Manners of such a Population.

LIKE you, I am a manufacturer for pecuniary profit. But having for many years acted on principles the reverse in many respects of those in which you have been instructed, and having found my procedure beneficial to others and to myself, even in a pecuniary point of view, I am anxious to explain such valuable principles, that you and those under your influence may equally partake of their advantages.

In two Essays, already published, I have developed some of these principles, and in the following pages you will find still more of them explained, with some detail of their application to practice, under the particular local circumstances in which I undertook the direction of the New Lanark Mills and Establishment.

By those details you will find, that from the commencement of my management I viewed the population, with the mechanism and every other part of the establishment, as a system composed of many parts, and which it was my duty and interest so to combine, as that every hand, as well as every spring, lever, and wheel, should effectually co-operate to produce the greatest pecuniary gain to the proprietors.

Many of you have long experienced in your manufacturing operations the advantages of substantial, well-contrived, and well-executed machinery.

Experience has also shown you the difference of the results between mechanism which is neat, clean, well arranged, and always in a high state of repair; and that which is allowed to be dirty, in disorder, without the means of preventing unnecessary friction, and which therefore becomes, and works, much out of repair.

In the first case, the whole economy and management are good; every operation proceeds with ease, order, and success. In the last, the reverse must follow, and a scene be presented of counteraction, confusion, and dissatisfaction among all the agents and instruments interested or occupied in the general process, which cannot fail to create great loss.

If then due care as to the state of your inanimate machines can produce such beneficial results, what may not be expected if you devote equal attention to your vital machines, which are far more wonderfully constructed?

When you shall acquire a right knowledge of these, of their curious mechanism, of their self-adjusting powers; when the proper main spring shall be applied to their varied movements, you will become conscious of their real value, and you will be readily induced to turn your thoughts more frequently from your inanimate to your living machines; you will discover that the latter may be easily trained and directed to procure a large increase of pecuniary gain, while you may also derive from them high and substantial gratification.

Will you then continue to expend large sums of money to procure the best devised mechanism of wood, brass, or iron; to retain it in perfect repair; to provide the best substance for the prevention of unnecessary friction, and to save it from falling into premature decay? Will you also devote years of intense application to understand the connexion of the various parts of these lifeless machines, to improve their effective powers, and to calculate with mathematical precision all their minute and combined movements? And when in these transactions you estimate time by minutes, and the money expended for the chance of increased gain by fractions, will you not afford some of your attention to consider whether a portion of your time and capital would not be more advantageously applied to improve your living machines?

From experience which cannot deceive me, I venture to assure you, that your time and money so applied, if directed by a true knowledge of the subject, would return you not five, ten, or fifteen per cent. for your capital so expended, but often fifty and in many cases a hundred per cent.

I have expended much time and capital upon improvements of the living machinery; and it will soon appear that the time and money so expended in the manufactory at New Lanark, even while such improvements are in progress only, and but half their beneficial effects attained, are now producing a return exceeding fifty per cent., and will shortly create profits equal to cent. per cent. on the original capital expended in them.

Indeed, after experience of the beneficial effects, from due care and attention to the mechanical implements, it became easy to a reflecting mind to conclude at once, that at least equal advantages would arise from the application of similar care and attention to the living instruments. And when it was perceived that inanimate mechanism was greatly improved by being made firm and substantial ; that it was the essence of economy to keep it neat, clean, regularly supplied with the best substance to prevent unnecessary friction, and, by proper provision for the purpose, to preserve it in good repair; it was natural to conclude that the more delicate, complex, living mechanism would be equally improved by being trained to strength and activity ; and that it would also prove true economy to keep it neat and clean; to treat it with kindness, that its mental movements might not experience too much irritating friction ; to endeavour by every means to make it more perfect; to supply it regularly with a sufficient quantity of wholesome food and other necessaries of life, that the body might be preserved in good working condition, and prevented from being out of repair, or falling prematurely to decay.

These anticipations are proved by experience to be just.

Since the general introduction of inanimate mechanism into British manufactories, man, with few exceptions, has been treated as a secondary and inferior machine; and far more attention has been given to perfect the raw materials of wood and metals than those of body and mind. Give but due reflection to the subject, and you will find that man, even as an instrument for the creation of wealth, may be still greatly improved.

But, my friends, a far more interesting and gratifying consideration remains. Adopt the means which ere long shall be rendered obvious to every understanding, and you may not only partially improve those living instruments, but learn how to impart to them such excellence as shall make them infinitely surpass those of the present and all former times.

Here then is an object which truly deserves your attention; and instead of devoting all your faculties to invent improved inanimate mechanism, let your thoughts be, at least in part, directed to discover how to combine the more excellent materials of body and mind, which, by a well-devised experiment, will be found capable of progressive improvement.

Thus seeing with the clearness of noon-day light, thus convinced with the certainty of conviction itself, let us not perpetuate the really unnecessary evils, which our present practices inflict on this large proportion of our fellow subjects. Should your pecuniary interests somewhat suffer by adopting the line of conduct now urged, many of you are so wealthy, that the expense of founding and continuing at your respective establishments the institutions necessary to improve your animate machines, would not be felt. But when you may have ocular demonstration that, instead of any pecuniary loss, a well-directed attention to form the character and increase the comforts of those who are so entirely at your mercy will essentially add to your gains, prosperity, and happiness; no reasons except those founded on ignorance of your self-interest, can in future prevent you from bestowing your chief care on the living machines which you employ; and by so doing you will prevent an accumulation of human misery, of which it is now difficult to form an adequate conception.

That you may be convinced of this most valuable truth, which due reflection will show you is founded on the evidence of unerring facts, is the sincere wish of

THE AUTHOR.

ESSAY THIRD.

A⊤ the conclusion of the Second Essay, a promise was made that an account should be given of the plans which were in progress at New Lanark for the further improvement of its inhabitants; and that a practical system should be sketched, by which equal advantages might be generally introduced among the poor and working classes throughout the United Kingdom.

This account became necessary, in order to exhibit even a limited view of the principles on which the plans of the author are founded, and to recommend them generally to practice.

That which has been hitherto done for the community of New Lanark, as described in the Second Essay, has chiefly consisted in WITHDRAWING SOME OF THOSE CIRCUMSTANCES WHICH TENDED TO GENERATE, CONTINUE, OR INCREASE EARLY BAD HABITS; THAT IS TO SAY, UNDOING THAT WHICH SOCIETY HAD FROM IGNORANCE PERMITTED TO BE DONE.

To effect this, however, was a far more difficult task than to train up a child from infancy in the way he should go, for that is the most easy process for the formation of character ; while to unlearn and to change long acquired habits, is a proceeding directly opposed to the most tenacious feelings of human nature.

Nevertheless the proper application steadily pursued did effect beneficial changes on these old habits, even beyond the most sanguine expectations of the party by whom the task was undertaken. The principles were derived from the study of human nature itself, and they could not fail of success.

Still, however, very little, comparatively speaking, had been done for them. They had not been taught the most valuable domestic and social habits : such as the most economical method of preparing food ; how to arrange their dwellings with neatness, and to keep them always clean and in order; but what was of infinitely more importance, they had not been instructed how to train their children, to form them into valuable members of the community, or to know that principles existed, which, when properly applied to practice from infancy, would insure from man to man, without chance of failure, a just, open, sincere, and benevolent conduct.

It was in this stage of the progress of improvement, that it became necessary to form arrangements for surrounding them with circumstances, which should gradually prepare the individuals to receive and firmly retain those domestic and social acquirements and habits.

For this purpose a building, which may be termed the " New Institution," was erected in the centre of the establishment, with an inclosed area before it. The area is intended for a playground for the children of the villagers, from the time they can walk alone until they enter the school.

It must be evident to those who have been in the practice of observing children with attention, that much of good or evil is taught to or acquired by a child at a very early period of its life ; that much of temper or disposition is correctly or incorrectly formed before he attains his second year; and that many durable impressions are made at the termination of the first twelve or even six months of his existence. The children therefore of the uninstructed and ill-instructed suffer material injury in the formation of their characters, during these and the subsequent years of childhood and of youth.

It was to prevent, or as much as possible to

counteract, these primary evils, to which the poor and working classes are exposed when infants, that the area became part of the New Institution.

Into this play-ground the children are to be received as soon as they can freely walk alone; to be superintended by persons instructed to take charge of them.

As the happiness of man chiefly, if not altogether, depends on his own sentiments and habits, as well as those of the individuals around him; and as any sentiments and habits may be given to all infants, it becomes of primary importance that those alone should be given to them which can contribute to their happiness. Each child therefore, on his entrance into the play-ground, is to be told in language which he can understand, that " he is never to injure his playfellows, but on the contrary he is to contribute all in his power to make them happy." This simple precept, when comprehended in all its bearings, and the habits which will arise from its early adoption into practice, *if no counteracting principles shall be forced on the young mind*, will effectually supersede all the errors which have hitherto kept the world in ignorance and misery. So simple a precept, too, will be

easily taught, and as easily acquired ; for the
chief employment of the Superintendant will
be to prevent any deviation from it in practice.
The older children, when they shall have experienced the endless advantages from acting on
this principle, will, by their example, soon enforce the practice of it on the young strangers;
and the happiness which the little groups will enjoy from this rational conduct, will insure its
speedy and general and willing adoption. The
habit also which they will acquire at this early
period of life, by continually acting on the principle, will fix it firmly ; it will become easy and
familiar to them, or, as it is often termed, natural.

Thus, by merely attending to the evidence of
our senses respecting human nature, and disre-
garding the wild, inconsistent, and absurd theories in which man has been hitherto trained in
all parts of the earth, we shall accomplish with
ease and certainty the supposed Herculean labour of forming a rational character in man, and
that too, chiefly, before the child commences the
ordinary course of education.

The character thus early formed will be as
durable as it will be advantageous to the individual and to the community ; for by the con-

stitution of our nature, when once the mind fully understands that which is true, the impression of that truth cannot be erased except by mental disease or death; while error must be relinquished at every period of life, whenever it can be made manifest to the mind in which it has been received. This part of the arrangement therefore will effect the following purposes:

The child will be removed, so far as is at present practicable, from the erroneous treatment of the yet untrained and untaught parents.

The parents will be relieved from the loss of time, and from the care and anxiety which are now occasioned by attendance on their children from the period when they can go alone to that at which they enter the school.

The child will be placed in a situation of safety, where, with its future schoolfellows and companions, it will acquire the best habits and principles, while at meal times and at night it will return to the caresses of its parents; and the affections of each are likely to be increased by the separation.

The area is also to be a place of meeting for the children from five to ten years of age, previous to and after school-hours, and to serve for a drill ground, the object of which will be hereafter explained. And a shade will be formed, under which, in stormy weather, the children may retire for shelter.

These are the important purposes to which a play-ground attached to a school may be applied.

Those who have derived a knowledge of human nature from observation know, that man in every situation requires relaxation from his constant and regular occupations, whatever they may be; and that, if he shall not be provided with or permitted to enjoy innocent and uninjurious amusements, he must and will partake of those which he can obtain, to give him temporary relief from his exertions, although the means of gaining that relief should be most pernicious. For man, irrationally instructed, is ever influenced far more by immediate feelings than by remote considerations.

Those, then, who desire to give mankind the character which it would be for the happiness of all that they should possess, will not fail to make careful provision for their amusement and recreation.

The Sabbath was originally so intended. It was instituted to be a day of universal enjoyment and happiness to the human race. It is frequently made, however, from the opposite extremes of error, either a day of superstitious gloom and tyranny over the mind, or of the most destructive intemperance and licentiousness. The one of these has been the cause of the other; the latter, the certain and natural consequences of the former. Relieve the human mind from useless and superstitious restraints, train it on those principles which facts, ascertained from the first knowledge of time to this day, demonstrate to be the only principles which are true, and intemperance and licentiousness will not exist; for such conduct in itself is neither the immediate nor the future interest of man; and he is ever governed by one or other of these considerations, according to the habits which have been given to him from infancy.

The Sabbath, in many parts of Scotland, is not now a day of innocent and cheerful recreation to the labouring man; nor can those who are confined all the week to sedentary occupations freely partake, without censure, of the air and exercise to which nature invites them, and which their health demands.

The errors of the times of superstition and bigotry still hold some sway, and compel those who wish to preserve a regard to their respectability in society to an overstrained demeanour; and this demeanour sometimes degenerates into hypocrisy, and is often the cause of great inconsistency. It is destructive of every open, honest, generous, and manly feeling. It disgusts many, and drives them to the opposite extreme. It is sometimes the cause of insanity. It is founded in ignorance, and defeats its own object.

While erroneous customs prevail in any country, it would evince an ignorance of human nature in any individual to offend against them, until he has convinced the community of their error.

To counteract, in some degree, the inconvenience which arose from this misapplication of the Sabbath, it became necessary to introduce on the other days of the week some innocent amusement and recreation for those whose labours were unceasing, and in winter almost uniform. In summer, the inhabitants of the village of New Lanark have their gardens and potatoe-grounds to cultivate; they have walks laid out to give them health, and the habit of being gratified with the ever-changing scenes of nature; for those scenes afford not only the most economical but also the most innocent pleasures which man can enjoy ; and all men may be easily trained to enjoy them,

In winter, the community are deprived of these healthy occupations and amusements; they are employed ten hours and three quarters every day in the week, except Sunday, and generally every individual continues during that time at the same work; and experience has shown that the average health and spirits of the community are several degrees lower in winter than in summer, and this in part may be fairly attributed to that cause.

These considerations suggested the necessity of rooms for innocent amusements and rational recreation.

Many well-intentioned individuals, unaccustomed to witness the conduct of those among the lower orders who have been rationally treated and trained, may fancy such an assemblage will necessarily become a scene of confusion and disorder: instead of which, however, it proceeds with uniform propriety; it is highly favourable to the health, spirits, and dispositions of the individuals so engaged; and if any irregularity should arise, the cause will be solely owing to the parties who attempt to direct the proceedings, being deficient in a practical knowledge of human nature.

It has been and ever will be found far more easy to lead mankind to virtue, or to rational conduct, by providing them with well-regulated innocent amusements and recreations, than by forcing them to submit to useless restraints, which tend only to create disgust, and often to connect such feelings even with that which is excellent in itself, merely because it has been injudiciously associated.

Hitherto indeed, in all ages, and in all countries, man seems to have blindly conspired against the happiness of man, and to have remained as ignorant of himself as he was of the solar system prior to the days of Copernicus and Galileo.

Many of the learned and wise among our ancestors were conscious of this ignorance, and deeply lamented its effects; and some of them recommended the partial adoption of those principles which can alone relieve the world from the miserable effects of ignorance.

The time, however, for the emancipation of the human mind was not then arrived, the world was not prepared to receive it. The history of humanity shows it to be an undeviating law of nature, that man shall not prematurely break the shell of ignorance; that he must patiently wait until the principle of knowledge has pervaded the whole mass of the interior, to give it life and strength sufficient to bear the light of day.

Those who have duly reflected on the nature and extent of the mental movements of the world for the last half century, must be conscious that great changes are in progress; that man is about to advance another important step towards that degree of intelligence which his natural powers seem capable of attaining. Observe the transactions of the passing hours; see the whole mass of mind in full motion; behold it momentarily increasing in vigour, and preparing ere long to burst its confinement. But what is to be the nature of this change? A due attention to the facts around us, and to those transmitted by the invention of printing from former ages, will afford a satisfactory reply.

From the earliest ages it has been the practice of the world, to act on the supposition that each individual man forms his own character, and that therefore he is accountable for all his sentiments and habits, and consequently merits reward for some, and punishment for others. Every system which has been established among men has been founded on these erroneous principles. When, however, they shall be brought to the test of fair examination, they will be found not only unsupported, but in direct opposition to all experience, and to the evidence of our senses. This is not a slight mistake which involves only trivial consequences; it is a fundamental error of the highest possible magnitude; it enters into all our proceedings regarding man from his infancy, and will be found to be the true and sole origin of evil. It generates and perpetuates ignorance, hatred, and revenge, where, without such error, only intelligence, confidence, and kindness would exist. It has hitherto been the Evil Genius of the world. It severs man from man throughout the various regions of the earth; and makes enemies of those who, but for this gross error, would have enjoyed each other's kind offices and sincere friendship. It is, in short, an error which carries misery in all its consequences.

This error cannot much longer exist; for every day will make it more and more evident THAT THE CHARACTER OF MAN IS, WITHOUT A SINGLE EXCEPTION, ALWAYS FORMED FOR HIM; THAT IT MAY BE, AND IS CHIEFLY, CREATED BY HIS PREDECESSORS; THAT THEY GIVE HIM, OR MAY GIVE HIM, HIS IDEAS AND HABITS, WHICH ARE THE POW-

ERS THAT GOVERN AND DIRECT HIS CON-
DUCT. MAN, THEREFORE, NEVER DID,
NOR IS IT POSSIBLE HE EVER CAN, FORM
HIS OWN CHARACTER.

The knowledge of this important fact has not
been derived from any of the wild and heated
speculations of an ardent and ungoverned imagination; on the contrary, it proceeds from a
long and patient study of the theory and practice of human nature, under many varied circumstances; it will be found to be a deduction
drawn from such a multiplicity of facts as to afford the most complete demonstration.

Had not mankind been misinstructed from
infancy on this subject, making it necessary that
they should unlearn what they have been taught,
the simple statement of this truth would render
it instantaneously obvious to every rational mind.
Men would know that their predecessors might
have given them the habits of ferocious canni-
balism, or of the highest known benevolence and
intelligence: and by the acquirement of this
knowledge they would soon learn that, as parents, preceptors, and legislators united, they
possess the means of training the rising generations to either of those extremes; that they
may with the greatest certainty make them the

conscientious worshippers of Juggernaut, or of the most pure spirit possessing the essence of every excellence which the human imagination can conceive; that they may train the young to become effeminate, deceitful, ignorantly self-ish, intemperate, revengeful, murderous,—of course ignorant, irrational, and miserable; or to be manly, just, generous, temperate, active, kind, and benevolent,—that is, intelligent, rational, and happy. The knowledge of these principles having been derived from facts which perpetually exist, they defy ingenuity itself to confute them; nay, the most severe scrutiny will make it evident that they are utterly unassailable.

Is it then wisdom to think and to act in opposition to the facts which hourly exhibit themselves around us, and in direct contradiction to the evidence of our senses? Inquire of the most learned and wise of the present day, ask them to speak with sincerity, and they will tell you that they have long known the principles on which society has been founded to be false. Hitherto, however, the tide of public opinion in all countries has been directed by a combination of prejudice, bigotry, and fanaticism, derived from the wildest imaginations of ignorance;

and the most enlightened men have not dared to expose those errors which to them were offensive, prominent, and glaring.

Happily for man, this reign of ignorance rapidly approaches to dissolution; its terrors are already on the wing, and soon they will be compelled to take their flight, never more to return. For now the knowledge of the existing errors is not only possessed. by the learned and reflecting, but it is spreading far and wide throughout society; and ere long it will be fully comprehended even by the most ignorant.

Attempts may indeed be made by individuals, who through ignorance mistake their real interests, to retard the progress of this knowledge; but as it will prove itself to be in unison with the evidence of our senses, and therefore true beyond the possibility of disproof, it cannot be impeded, and in its course will overwhelm all opposition.

These principles, however, are not more true in theory than beneficial in practice whenever they are properly applied. Why, then, should all their substantial advantages be longer withheld from the mass of mankind? Can it, by possibility, be a crime to pursue the only practical means which a rational being can adopt to diminish the misery of man, and increase his happiness?

These questions, of the deepest interest to society, are now brought to the fair test of public experiment. It remains to be proved, whether the character of man shall continue to be formed under the guidance of the most inconsistent notions, the errors of which for centuries past have been manifest to every reflecting rational mind; or whether it shall be moulded under the direction of uniformly consistent principles, derived from the unvarying facts of the creation; principles, the truth of which no sane man will now attempt to deny.

It is then by the full and complete disclosure of these principles, that the destruction of ignorance and misery is to be effected, and the reign of reason, intelligence, and happiness, is to be firmly established.

It was necessary to give this developement of the principles advocated, that the remaining parts of the New Institution, yet to be described, may be clearly understood. We now proceed to explain the several purposes intended to be accomplished by the School, Lecture-room, and Church.

It must be evident to those who have any

powers of reason yet undestroyed, that man is
now taught and trained in a theory and practice
directly opposed to each other. Hence the
perpetual inconsistencies, follies and absurdities,
which every one can readily discover in his
neighbour, without being conscious that he also
possesses similar incongruities. The instruction
to be given in the School, Lecture-Room, and
Church, is intended to counteract and remedy
the evil; and to prove the incalculable advantages which society would derive from the introduction of a theory and practice consistent
with each other. The uppermost story of the
New Institution is arranged to serve for a School,
Lecture-room, and Church. And these are intended to have a direct influence in forming the
character of the villagers.

It is comparatively of little avail to give to
either young or old " precept upon precept, and
line upon line," EXCEPT THE MEANS SHALL
BE ALSO PREPARED TO TRAIN THEM IN
GOOD PRACTICAL HABITS. Hence an education for the untaught and ill-taught becomes of
the first importance to the welfare of society:
and it is this which has influenced all the arrangements connected with the New Institution.

The time the children will remain under the discipline of the play-ground and school will afford all the opportunity that can be desired, to create, cultivate, and establish those habits and sentiments which tend to the welfare of the individual and of the community. And in conformity to this plan of proceeding, the precept which was given to the child of two years old, on coming into the play-ground, "that he must endeavour to make his companions happy," is to be renewed and enforced on his entrance into the school; and the first duty of the Schoolmaster will be to train his pupils to acquire the practice of always acting on this principle. It is a simple rule, the plain and obvious reasons for which, children at an early age may be readily taught to comprehend : as they advance in years, become familiarised with its practice, and experience the beneficial effects to themselves, they will better feel and understand all its important consequences to society.

Such then being the foundation on which the practical habits of the children are to be formed, we proceed to explain the superstructure.

In addition to the knowledge of the principle and practice of the abovementioned precept, the boys and girls are to be taught in the school to read well, and to understand what they read; to write expeditiously a good legible hand; and to learn correctly, so that they may comprehend, and use with facility, the fundamental rules of arithmetic. The girls are also to be taught to sew, cut out and make up useful family garments; and after acquiring a sufficient knowledge of these, they are to attend in rotation in the public kitchen and eating-rooms; to learn to prepare wholesome food in an œconomical manner, and to keep a house neat and well arranged.

It was said that the children are to be taught to read well, and to understand what they read.

In many schools, the children of the poor and labouring classes are never taught to understand what they read; the time therefore which is occupied in the mockery of instruction is lost; in other schools, the children, through the ignorance of their instructors, are taught to believe without reasoning, and thus never to think or to reason correctly. These truly lamentable practices cannot fail to indispose the young mind for plain, simple, and rational instruction.

The books by which it is now the common custom to teach children to read, inform them of any thing except that which, at their age, they ought to be taught: hence the inconsistencies and follies of adults. It is full time that this system should be changed. *Can man, when possessing the full vigour of his faculties, form a rational judgement on any subject, until he has first collected all the facts respecting it, which are known? Has not this ever been, and will not this ever remain, the only path by which human knowledge can be obtained?* Then children ought to be instructed on the same principles. They should first be taught the knowledge of facts, commencing with those which are the most familiar to the young mind, and gradually proceeding to the most useful and necessary to be known by the respective individuals in the rank of life in which they are likely to be placed; and in all cases the children should have as clear an explanation of each fact as their minds can comprehend, rendering those explanations more detailed as the child acquires strength and capacity of intellect.

As soon as the young mind shall be duly prepared for such instruction, the master should not allow any opportunity to escape, that would enable him to enforce the clear and inseparable connection which exists between the interest and happiness of each individual, and the interest and happiness of every other individual. This should be the beginning and end of all his instruction: and by degrees it will be so well understood by his pupils, that they will receive the same conviction of its truth, that those familiar with mathematics now entertain of the demonstrations of Euclid. And when thus comprehended, the all-prevailing principle of known life, the desire of happiness, will compel them without deviation to pursue it in practice.

It is much to be regretted that the strength and capacity of the minds of children are yet unknown: their faculties have been hitherto estimated by the folly of the instruction which has been given to them; while, if they were never taught to acquire error, they would speedily exhibit such powers of mind, as would convince the most incredulous how much human intellect has been injured by the ignorance of former and present treatment.

It is therefore indeed important that the mind from its birth should receive those ideas only, which are consistent with each other, which are in unison with all the known facts of the creation, and which are therefore true. Now, however, from the day they are born, the minds of children are impressed with false notions of themselves and of mankind ; and in lieu of be-

ing conducted into the plain path leading to
health and to happiness, the utmost pains are
taken to compel them to pursue an opposite direction, in which they can attain only inconsistency and error.

Let the plan which has now been recommended, be steadily put in practice from infancy,
*without counteraction from the systems of edu-
cation which now exist;* and characters even in
youth may be formed, that in true knowledge,
and in every good and valuable quality, will not
only greatly surpass the wise and learned of the
present and preceding times, but appear, as they
really will be, a race of rational, or superior beings. It is true, this change cannot be instantaneously established; it cannot be created by
magic, or by a miracle; it must be effected
gradually—and to accomplish it finally, will
prove a work of labour and of years. For
those who have been misinstructed from infancy, who have now influence, and are active
in the world, and whose activity is directed by
the false notions of their forefathers, will of
course endeavour to obstruct the change. Those
who have been systematically impressed with
early errors, and conscientiously think them to
be truths, will of necessity, while such errors

remain, endeavour to perpetuate them in their children. Some simple but general method, therefore, becomes necessary to counteract as speedily as possible an evil of so formidable a magnitude.

It was this view of the subject which suggested the utility of preparing the means to admit of evening lectures in the New Institution; and it is intended they should be given, during winter, three nights in the week, alternately with dancing.

To the ill-trained and ill-taught these lectures may be made invaluable; and these are now numerous; for the far greater part of the population of the world has been permitted to pass the proper season of instruction without being trained to be rational; and they have acquired only the ideas and habits which proceed from ignorant association and erroneous instruction.

It is intended that the lectures should be familiar discourses, delivered in plain impressive language, to instruct the adult part of the community in the most useful practical parts of knowledge in which they are deficient, particularly in the proper method of training their children to become rational creatures; how to expend the earnings of their own labour to advantage; and how to appropriate the surplus gains which will be left to them, in order to create a fund which will relieve them from the anxious fear of future want, and thus give them, under the many errors of the present systems, that rational confidence in their own exertions and good conduct, without which, consistency of character or domestic comfort cannot be obtained, and ought not to be expected. The young people may be also questioned relative to their progress in useful knowledge, and allowed to ask for explanations. In short, these lectures may be made to convey, in an amusing and agreeable manner, highly valuable and substantial information to those who are now the most ignorant in the community; and by similar means, which at a trifling expense may be put into action over the whole kingdom, the most important benefits may be given to the labouring classes, and, through them, to the whole mass of society.

For it should be considered, that *the far greater part of the population belong to or have risen from the labouring classes; and by them the happiness and comfort of all ranks, not excluding the highest, are very essentially influenced;* because even much more of the character of children in all families is formed by the servants, than is ever supposed by those unaccustomed to trace with attention the human mind from earliest infancy. It is indeed impossible that children in any situation can be correctly trained, until those who surround them from infancy shall be previously well instructed: and the value of good servants may be duly appreciated by those who have experienced the difference between the very good and very bad.

The last part of the intended arrangement of the New Institution remains yet to be described. This is the church and its doctrines; and they involve considerations of the highest interest and importance; inasmuch as a knowledge of truth on the subject of religion would permanently establish the happiness of man; for it is the inconsistencies alone, proceeding from the want of this knowledge, which have created, and still create, a great proportion of the miseries which exist in the world.

The only certain criterion of truth is, that it is ever consistent with itself; it remains one and the same, under every view and comparison of it which can be made; while error will not stand the test of this investigation and comparison, because it ever leads to absurd conclusions.

Those whose minds are equal to the subject will, ere this, have discovered that the principles in which mankind have been hitherto instructed, and by which they have been governed, will not bear the test of this criterion. Investigate and compare them: they betray absurdity, folly, and weakness; hence the infinity of jarring opinions, dissentions, and miseries, which have hitherto prevailed.

Had any one of the various opposing systems which have governed the world, and disunited man from man, been true, without any mixture of error,—that system, very speedily after its public promulgation, would have pervaded society, and compelled all men to have acknowledged its truth.

The criterion however which has been stated shows that they are all, without an exception, in part inconsistent with the works of nature; that is, with the facts which exist around us. Those systems therefore must have contained some fundamental errors; and it is utterly impossible for man to become rational, or enjoy the happiness which he is capable of attaining, until those errors are exposed and annihilated.

Each of those systems contains some truth with more error: hence it is that no one of them has gained, or is likely to gain, universality.

The truth which the several systems posse*s,
serves to cover and perpetuate the errors which
they contain; but those errors are most obvious
to all those who have not, from infancy, been
taught to receive them.

Is proof demanded? Ask, in succession, those
who are esteemed the most intelligent and enlightened of every sect and party, what is their
opinion of every other sect and party throughout
the world. Is it not evident that, without one
exception, the answer of each will be, that they
all contain errors so clearly in opposition to reason and to equity, that he can feel only pity and
deep commiseration for the individuals whose
minds have been thus perverted and rendered
irrational? And this reply they will all make,
unconscious that they themselves are of the number whom they commiserate.

The doctrines which have been taught to every
known sect, combined with the external circumstances by which they have been surrounded,
have been directly calculated, and could not fail,
to produce the characters which have existed.
And the doctrines in which the inhabitants of
the world are now instructed, combined with the
external circumstances by which they are surrounded, form the characters which at present
pervade society.

The doctrines which have been and now are taught throughout the world must necessarily create and perpetuate, and they do create and perpetuate, a total want of mental charity among men. They also generate superstition, bigotry, hypocrisy, hatred, revenge, wars, and all their evil consequences. For it has been and is a fundamental principle in every system hitherto taught, with exceptions more nominal than real, " That man will possess merit, and receive eternal reward, by believing the doctrines of that peculiar system ; that he will be eternally punished if he disbelieves them ; that all those innumerable individuals also, who, through time, have not been taught to believe other than the tenets of this system, must be doomed to eternal misery." Yet nature itself, in all its works, is perpetually operating to convince man of such gross absurdities.

Yes, my deluded fellow-men, believe me, for your future happiness, that the facts around us, when you shall observe them aright, will make it evident even to demonstration, that all such doctrines must be erroneous, because THE WILL OF MAN HAS NO POWER WHATEVER OVER HIS OPINIONS ; HE MUST, AND EVER DID, AND EVER WILL, BELIEVE WHAT HAS BEEN, IS, OR MAY BE IMPRESSED ON HIS MIND

BY HIS PREDECESSORS, AND THE CIRCUM-
STANCES WHICH SURROUND HIM. It becomes therefore the essence of irrationality to
suppose that any human being, from the creation to this day, could deserve praise or blame,
reward or punishment, for the prepossession of
early education.

It is from these fundamental errors in all systems which have been hitherto taught to the
mass of mankind, that the misery of the human
race has to so great an extent proceeded; for,
in consequence of it, man has been always instructed from infancy to believe impossibilities;
he is still taught to pursue the same insane course,
and the result still is misery. Let this source
of wretchedness, this most lamentable of all errors, this scourge of the human race, be publicly
exposed ; and let those just principles be introduced, which prove themselves true by their uniform consistency and the evidence of our senses:
hence insincerity, hatred, revenge, and even a
wish to injure a fellow-creature, will ere long
be unknown ; and mental charity, heartfelt benevolence, and acts of kindness to one another,
will be the distinguishing characteristics of human nature.

Shall then misery most complicated and extensive be experienced, from the prince to the peasant, in all nations throughout the world, and shall its cause and prevention be known, and yet withheld? The knowledge of this cause, however, cannot be communicated to mankind without offending against the deep-rooted prejudices of all. The work is therefore replete with difficulties, which can alone be overcome by those who, foreseeing all its important practical advantages, may be induced to contend against them.

Yet, difficult as it may be to establish this grand truth generally throughout society, on account of the dark and gross errors in which the world to this period has been instructed, it will be found, whenever the subject shall undergo a full investigation, that the principles now brought forward cannot, by possibility, injure any class of men, or even a single individual. On the contrary, there is not one member of the great family of the world, from the highest to the lowest, that will not derive the most important benefits from its public promulgation. And when such incalculable, substantial, and permanent advantages are clearly seen and strongly felt, shall individual considerations be for a moment put in competition with its attainment?

No! Ease, comfort, the good opinion of a part of society, and even life itself, may be sacrificed to those prejudices; and yet the principles on which this knowledge is founded must ultimately and universally prevail.

This high event, of unequalled magnitude in the history of humanity, is thus confidently predicted, because the knowledge whence that confidence proceeds is not derived from any of the uncertain legends of the days of dark and gross ignorance, but from the plain and obvious facts which now exist throughout the world. Due attention to these facts, to these truly revealed works of nature, will soon instruct, or rather compel, mankind to discover the universal errors in which they have been trained.

The principle then on which the doctrines taught in the New Institution are proposed to be founded, is, that they shall be in unison with universally revealed facts which cannot but be true.

The following are some of the facts which, with a view to this part of the undertaking, may be deemed fundamental.

That man is born with a desire to obtain happiness, which desire is the primary cause of all his actions, continues through life, and, in popular language, is called self-interest.

That he is also born with the germs of animal propensities, or the desire to sustain, enjoy, and propagate life ; and which desires, as they grow and develope themselves, are termed his natural inclinations.

That he is born likewise with faculties, which in their growth receive, convey, compare, and become conscious of receiving and comparing, ideas.

That the ideas so received, conveyed, compared, and understood, constitute human knowledge, or mind, which acquires strength and maturity with the growth of the individual.

That the desire of happiness in man, the germs of his natural inclinations, and the faculties by which he acquires knowledge, are formed, unknown to himself, in the womb ; and, whether perfect or imperfect, they are alone the immediate work of the Creator, and over which the infant and future man have no control.

That these inclinations and faculties are not formed exactly alike in any two individuals : hence the diversity of talents, and the varied impressions called liking, and disliking, which the same external objects make on different persons, and the lesser varieties which exist among men whose characters have been formed apparently under similar circumstances.

That the knowledge which man receives, is derived from the objects around him, and chiefly from the example and instruction of his immediate predecessors.

That this knowledge may be limited or extended, erroneous or true; limited when the individual receives few, and extended when he receives many, ideas; erroneous when those ideas are inconsistent with the facts which exist around him, and true when they are uniformly consistent with them.

That the misery which he experiences, and the happiness which he enjoys, depend on the kind and degree of knowledge which he receives, and on that which is possessed by those around him.

That when the knowledge which he receives is true, and unmixed with error, although it be limited, if the community in which he lives possesses the same kind and degree of knowledge, he will enjoy happiness in proportion to the extent of that knowledge. On the contrary, when the opinions which he receives are erroneous, and the opinions possessed by the community in which he resides are equally erroneous, his misery will be in proportion to the extent of those erroneous opinions.

That when the knowledge which man receives

shall be extended to its utmost limit, and true without any mixture of error, then he may and will enjoy all the happiness of which his nature will be capable.

That it consequently becomes of the first and highest importance that man should be taught to distinguish truth from error.

That man has no other means of discovering what is false, except by his faculty of reason, or power of acquiring and comparing the ideas which he receives.

That when this faculty is properly cultivated or trained from infancy, and the child is rationally instructed to retain no impressions or ideas which by his powers of comparing them appear to be inconsistent, then the individual will acquire real knowledge, or those ideas only which will leave an impression of their consistency, or truth, on all minds which have not been rendered irrational by an opposite procedure.

That the reasoning faculty may be injured and destroyed, during its growth, by reiterated impressions being made upon it of notions not derived from realities, and which it therefore cannot compare with the ideas previously received from the objects around it. And when the mind receives these notions which it cannot compre-

hend, along with those ideas which it is conscious
are true and yet inconsistent with such notions,
then the reasoning faculties become injured, the
individual is taught or forced to believe, and not
to think or reason, and partial insanity or defective powers of judging ensue.

That all men are thus erroneously trained at
present, and hence the inconsistences and misery
of the world.

That the fundamental errors now impressed
from infancy on the minds of all men, and from
whence all their other errors proceed, are, that
they form their own individual characters, and
possess merit or demerit for the peculiar notions
impressed on the mind during its early growth,
before they have acquired strength and experience to judge of or resist the impressions of
those notions or opinions, which on investigation
appear contradictions to facts existing around
them, and which are therefore false.

That these false notions have ever produced
evil and misery in the world, and that they still
disseminate them in every direction.

That the sole cause of their existence hitherto
has been man's ignorance of human nature;
while their consequences have been, all the evil
and misery, except those of accidents, disease,

and death, with which man has been and is afflicted ; and that the evil and misery which arise from accidents, disease, and death, are also greatly increased and extended by man's ignorance of himself.

That in proportion as man's desire of self-happiness, or his self-love, is directed by true knowledge, those actions will abound which are virtuous and beneficial to man; that in proportion as it is influenced by false notions, or the absence of true knowledge, those actions will prevail which generate crimes, from whence arises an endless variety of misery ; and consequently that every rational means should be now adopted to detect error and increase true knowledge among men.

That when these truths are made evident, every individual will necessarily endeavour to promote the happiness of every other individual within his sphere of action ; because he must clearly, and without any doubt, comprehend such conduct to be the essence of self-interest, or the true cause of self-happiness.

Here then is a firm foundation on which to erect vital religion, pure and undefiled, and the only one which, without any counteracting evil, can give peace and happiness to man.

It is to bring into practical operation, in forming the characters of men, these most important of all truths, that the religious part of the Institution at New Lanark will be chiefly directed; and such are the fundamental principles upon which the Instructor will proceed.

They are thus publicly avowed before all men, that they may undergo discussion, and the most severe scrutiny and investigation.

Let those, therefore, who are esteemed the most learned and wise throughout the various states and empires of the world, examine them to their foundation, compare them with every fact which exists ; and if the shadow of inconsistency or falsehood be discovered, let it be publicly exposed, that error may not more abound.

But should they withstand this extended ordeal, and prove themselves uniformly consistent with every known fact, and therefore true; then let it be declared, that man may be permitted by man to become rational, and that the misery of the world may be speedily removed.

Having alluded to the chief uses of the play-ground and exercise-rooms, with the School, Lecture-room, and Church, it remains, to complete the account of the New Institution, that the object of the drill exercise, mentioned when stating the purposes of the play-ground, should be explained; and to this we proceed.

Were all men trained to be rational, the art of war would be rendered useless. While, however, any part of mankind shall be taught that they form their own characters, and continue to be trained from infancy to think and act irrationally; that is, to acquire feelings of enmity, and to deem it a duty to engage in war, against those who have been instructed to differ from them in sentiments and habits; even the most rational must, for their personal security, learn the means of defence; and every community of such characters, while surrounded by men who have been thus improperly taught, should acquire a knowledge of this destructive art, that they may be enabled to overrule the actions of irrational beings, and maintain peace.

To accomplish these objects to the utmost practical limit, and with the least inconvenience, every male should be instructed how best to defend, when attacked, the community to which he belongs. And these advantages are only to be obtained by providing proper means for the instruction of all boys in the use of arms and the arts of war.

As an example how easily and effectually this

might be accomplished over the British Isles, it is intended that the boys trained and educated in the Institution at New Lanark shall be thus instructed; that the person appointed to attend the children in the play-ground shall be qualified to drill and teach the boys the manual exercise, and that he shall be frequently so employed. That afterwards fire-arms, of proportionate weight and size to the age and strength of the boys, shall be provided for them; when also they might be taught to practise and understand the more complicated military movements.

This exercise, properly administered, will greatly contribute to the health and spirits of the boys, give them an erect and proper form, and habits of attention, celerity, and order. They will however be taught to consider this exercise an art rendered absolutely necessary by the partial insanity of some of their fellow-creatures, who, by the errors of their predecessors transmitted through preceding generations, have been taught to acquire feelings of enmity increasing to madness against those who could not avoid differing from them in sentiments and habits; that this art should never be brought into practice except to restrain the violence of

such madmen; and in these cases that it should
be administered with the least possible severity;
and solely to prevent the evil consequences of
those rash actions of the insane, and if possible
cure them of their disease.

Thus, in a few years, by foresight and arrangement, may almost the whole expense and inconvenience attending the local military be super-
seded, and a permanent force created, which in
numbers, discipline, and principles, would be
superior beyond all comparison for the purposes
of defence, always ready in case of need, yet
without the loss which is now sustained by the
community of efficient and valuable labour.
The expenditure which would be saved by this
simple expedient would be far more than competent to educate the whole of the poor and labouring classes of these kingdoms.

There is still another arrangement in contemplation for the community at New Lanark, and
without which the establishment will remain in-
complete.

It is an expedient to enable the individuals,
by their own foresight, prudence, and industry,
to secure to themselves in old age a comfortable
provision and asylum.

Those now employed at the establishment contribute to a fund which supports them when too ill to work, or when superannuated. This fund, however, is not calculated to give them more than a bare existence; and it is surely desirable that, after they have spent nearly half a century in unremitting industry, they should, if possible, in the decline of life, enjoy a comfortable independence.

To effect this object, it is intended that in the most pleasant situation near the present village, neat and convenient dwellings should be erected, with gardens attached ; that they should be surrounded and sheltered by plantations, through which public walks should be formed, and the whole arranged to give the occupiers the most substantial comforts.

That these dwellings, with the privileges of the public walks, &c. shall become the property of those individuals who, without compulsion, shall subscribe such equitable sums monthly as, in a given number of years, will be equal to their purchase, and to create a fund from which, when these individuals become occupiers of their new residences, they may receive weekly, monthly, or quarterly payments sufficient for their support, the expenses of which may be reduced to a very low rate individually, by arrangements

which may be easily formed to supply all their
wants with little trouble to themselves; and by
their previous instruction they will be enabled
to afford the small additional subscription which
will be required for these purposes.

This part of the arrangement would always
present a prospect of rest, comfort, and happiness to those employed: in consequence their
daily occupations would be performed with more
spirit and cheerfulness, and their labour would
appear comparatively light and easy. Those
still engaged in active operations would of course
frequently visit their former companions and
friends, who after having spent their years of
toil were in the actual enjoyment of this simple
retreat; and from this intercourse each party
would naturally derive pleasure. The reflections
of each would be most gratifying. The old
would rejoice that they had been trained in habits
of industry, temperance, and foresight, to enable
them to receive and enjoy in their declining
years every reasonable comfort which the present state of society will admit; the young and
middle-aged, that they were pursuing the same
course ; and that they had not been trained to
waste their money, time, and health, in idleness
and intemperance. These and many similar re-

flections could not fail often to arise in their minds; and those who could look forward with confident hopes to such certain comfort and independence would, in part, enjoy by anticipation these advantages. In short, when this part of the arrangement is well considered, it will be found to be most important to the community and to the proprietors: indeed, the extensively good effects of it will be experienced in such a variety of ways, that to describe them even below the truth would appear an extravagant exaggeration. They will not however prove the less true because mankind are yet ignorant of the practice, and of the principles on which it has been founded.

These, then, are the plans which are in progress or intended for the further improvement of the inhabitants of New Lanark: they have uniformly proceeded from the principles which have been developed through these Essays, restrained however, hitherto, in their operations by the local sentiments and unfounded notions of the community and neighbourhood, and by the peculiar circumstances of the establishment.

In every measure to be introduced at the place in question, for the comfort and happiness of man, the existing errors of the country were always to be considered ; and as the establishment belonged to parties whose views were various, it became also necessary to devise means to create pecuniary gains from each improvement sufficient to satisfy the spirit of commerce.

All therefore which has been done for the happiness of this community, which consists of between two and three thousand individuals, is far short of what might have been easily effected in practice, had not mankind been previously trained in error. Hence, in devising these plans, the sole consideration was not what were the measures, dictated by these principles, which would produce the greatest happiness to man ; but what could be effected in practice under the present irrational systems by which these proceedings were surrounded.

Imperfect however as these proceedings must yet be, in consequence of the formidable obstructions enumerated, they will yet appear, upon a full and minute investigation by minds equal to the comprehension of such a system, to combine a greater degree of substantial comfort to the individuals employed in the manufactory, and of pecuniary profit to the proprietors, than has hitherto been found attainable.

But to whom can such arrangements be sub-

mitted? Not to the mere commercial character, in whose estimation to forsake the path of
immediate individual gain would be to show
symptoms of a disordered imagination; for the
children of commerce have been trained to direct all their faculties to buy cheap and sell dear;
and consequently those who are the most expert
and successful in this wise and noble art are in
the commercial world deemed to possess foresight and superior acquirements, while such as
attempt to improve the moral habits and increase the comforts of those whom they employ
are termed wild enthusiasts.

Nor yet are they to be submitted to the mere
men of the law; for they are necessarily trained
to endeavour to make wrong appear right, or involve both in a maze of intricacies, and to legalize injustice. Nor to mere political leaders
or their partisans; for they are embarrassed by
the trammels of party, which mislead their judgement, and often constrain them to sacrifice the
real well-being of the community and of themselves to an apparent but most mistaken self-interest.

Nor to those termed heroes and conquerors,
or their followers; for their minds have been
trained to consider the infliction of human mi-

sery, and the commission of military murders, a glorious duty, almost beyond reward.

Nor yet to the fashionable or splendid in their appearance; for these are from infancy trained to deceive and to be deceived; to accept shadows for substances; and to live a life of insincerity, and consequent discontent and misery.

Still less are they to be exclusively submitted to the official expounders and defenders of the various opposing religious systems throughout the world; for many of these are actively engaged in propagating imaginary notions, which cannot fail to vitiate the rational powers of man, and perpetuate his misery.

These principles therefore, and the practical systems which they recommend, are not to be submitted to the judgement of those who have been trained under and continue in any of these unhappy combinations of circumstances; but they are to be submitted to the dispassionate and patient investigation and decision of those individuals of every rank and class and denomination in society, who have become in some degree conscious of the errors in which they exist; who have felt the thick mental darkness by which they are surrounded; who are ardently desirous of discovering and following truth wherever it may lead; and who can perceive the inseparable connection which exists between individual and general, between private and public good!

It has been said, and it is now repeated, that these principles, thus combined, will prove themselves unerringly true against the most insidious or open attack; and ere long they will, by their irresistible truth, pervade society to the utmost bounds of the earth; for " silence will not retard their progress, and opposition will give increased celerity to their movements." When they shall have dissipated in some degree, as they speedily will dissipate, the thick darkness in which the human mind has been and is still enveloped, the endless beneficial consequences which must follow the general introduction of them into practice may then be explained in greater detail, and urged upon minds to which they will then appear less questionable. In the mean time we shall proceed to state, in a fourth Essay, of what immediate improvements the present state of the British population is susceptible in practice.

ESSAY FOURTH.

THE PRINCIPLES OF THE FORMER ESSAYS

APPLIED TO

Government.

It is beyond all comparison better to prevent than to punish crimes.

A System of Government therefore which shall prevent ignorance, and consequently crime, will be infinitely superior to one, which, by encouraging the first, creates a necessity for the last, and afterwards inflicts punishment on both.

ESSAY FOURTH.

THE end of government is to make the governed and the governors happy.

That government then is the best, which in practice produces the greatest happiness to the greatest number; including those who govern, and those who obey.

In a former Essay we said, and it admits of practical demonstration, that by adopting the proper means, man may, by degrees, be trained to live in any part of the world without poverty, without crime, and without punishment; for all these are the effects of error in the various systems of training and governing; error, proceeding from very gross ignorance of human nature.

It is of primary importance to make this ignorance manifest, and to show what are the means which are endowed with that transcendent efficacy.

We have also said that man may be trained to acquire any sentiments and habits, or any character; and no one now, possessing pretensions to the knowledge of human nature, will deny that the government of any independent community may form the individuals of that community into the best, or into the worst characters.

If there be one duty therefore more imperative than another, on the government of every country, it is, that it should adopt, without delay, the proper means to form those sentiments and habits in the people, which shall give the most permanent and substantial advantages to the individuals and to the community.

Survey the acquirements of the earliest ages; trace the progress of those acquirements, through all the subsequent periods, to the present hour; and say if there be any thing of real value in them, except that which contributes in practice to increase the happiness of the world.

And yet, with all the parade of learning contained in the myriads of volumes which have been written, and which still daily pour from the press, the knowledge of the first step of the progress which leads to human happiness remains yet unknown, or disregarded by the mass of mankind.

The important knowledge to which we allude is, " That the old collectively may train the young collectively, to be ignorant and miserable, or to be intelligent and happy." And, on investigation, this will be found to be one of those simple yet grand laws of the universe which experience discovers and confirms, and which, as soon as men become familiar with it, will no longer admit of denial or dispute. Fortunate will be that government which shall first acquire this knowledge in theory, and adopt it in practice.

To obtain its introduction into our own country first, a mode of procedure is now submitted to the immediate governing powers of the British Empire; and it is so submitted with an ardent desire that it may undergo the most full and ample discussion; that if it shall, as on investigation it will, be found to be the only consistent, and therefore rational, system of conducting human beings, it may be temperately and progressively introduced, instead of those defective national practices by which the state is now governed.

We therefore proceed to explain how this principle may now be introduced into practice, without injury to any part of society. For it is the time and manner of introducing this principle, and its consequent practice, which alone constitute any difficulty.

This will appear evident, when it is considered that, although, from a plain statement of the most simple facts, the truth of the principle cannot fail to prove so obvious that no one will ever attempt openly to attack it ; and although its adoption into practice will speedily accumulate benefits of which the world can now form no adequate conception: yet both theory and practice are to be introduced into a society, trained and matured under principles that have impressed upon the individuals who compose it the most opposite habits and sentiments; which have been so entwined from infancy in their bodily and mental growth, that the simplicity and irresistible power of truth alone can disentangle them, and expose their fallacy. It becomes then necessary, to prevent the evils of a too sudden change, that those who have been thus nursed in ignorance may be progressively removed from the abodes of mental darkness, to the intellectual light which this principle cannot fail to produce. The light of true knowledge therefore must be first made to dawn on those dwellings of darkness, and afterwards gradually to increase, as it can be borne by the opening faculties of their inhabitants.

To proceed on this plan, it becomes necessary

to direct our attention to the actual state of the British population ; to disclose the cause of those great and leading evils of which all now complain.

It will then be seen that the foundation on which these evils have been erected is ignorance, proceeding from the errors which have been impressed on the minds of the present generation by its predecessors ; and chiefly by that *greatest of all errors, the notion, that individuals form their own characters.* For while this most inconsistent and therefore most absurd of all human conceptions shall continue to be forced upon the young mind, there will remain no foundation whatever on which to build a sincere love and extended charity from man to his fellow-creatures.

But destroy this hydra of human calamity, this immolator of every principle of rationality; this monster, which hitherto has effectually guarded every avenue that can lead to true benevolence and active kindness, and human happiness will be speedily established on a rock from whence it shall never more be removed.

This enemy of humanity may now be most easily destroyed. Let it be dragged forth from beneath the dark mysterious veil by which, till now, it has been hid from the eyes of the world; expose it but for an instant to the clear light of intellectual day; and, as though conscious of its own deformity, it will instantaneously vanish, never to reappear.

As a ground-work then of a rational system, let this absurd doctrine, and all the chain of consequences which follow from it, be withdrawn, and let that only be taught as sacred, which can be demonstrated by its never-failing consistency to be true.

This essential object being accomplished, and accomplished it must be before another step can be taken to form man into a rational being, the next is to withdraw those national laws which chiefly emanate from that erroneous doctrine, and now exist in full vigour; training the population to almost every kind of crime. For these laws are, without chance of failure, adapted to produce a long train of crimes, which crimes are accordingly produced.

Some of the most prominent to which allusion is made are such as encourage the consumption of ardent spirits, by fostering and extending those receptacles to seduce the ignorant and wretched, called gin-shops and pot-houses;— those which sanction and legalize gambling among the poor, under the name of a state lottery;—those which are insidiously destroying the real strength of the country under the name of providing for the poor;—and those of punishment, which, under the present irrational system of legislation, are supposed to be absolutely necessary to hold society together.

To prove the accuracy of this deduction, millions of facts exist around us, speaking in a language so clearly connected and audible, that it is scarcely credible any man can misunderstand it.

These facts proclaim aloud to the universe, that ignorance generates, fosters, and multiplies sentiments and actions which must produce private and public misery; and that when evils are experienced, instead of withdrawing the *cause* which created them, it invents and applies punishments, which, to a superficial observer, may appear to lessen the evils which afflict society, while, in reality, they greatly increase them.

Intelligence, on the contrary, traces to its source the cause of every evil which exists; adopts the proper measures to remove the *cause;* and then, with the most unerring confidence, rests satisfied that its object will be accomplished.

Thus then intelligence, or, in other words, plain unsophisticated reason, will consider the various sentiments and actions which now create misery in society, will patiently trace the cause whence those sentiments and actions proceed, and immediately apply the proper remedies to remove them.

And attention, thus directed, discovers that the cause of such sentiments and actions in the British population is the laws which have been enumerated, and others which shall be hereafter noticed.

To withdraw therefore the existing evils which afflict society, these unwise laws must be progressively repealed or modified. The British constitution, in its present outline, is admirably adapted to effect these changes, without the evils which always accompany a coerced or ill-prepared change.

As a preliminary step, however, to the commencement of national improvements, it should be declared with a sincerity which shall not admit of any after deviation, that no individual of the present generation should be deprived of the emolument which he now receives, or of that which has been officially or legally promised.

The next step in national reform is to with

draw from the national church those tenets which constitute its weakness and create its danger. Yet still, to prevent the evils of any premature change, let the church in other respects remain as it is; because under the old established forms it may effect the most valuable purposes.

To render it truly a national church, all tests, as they are called, that is, declarations of belief in which all cannot conscientiously join, should be withdrawn: this alteration would tend more perhaps than any other which can be devised, to give stability both to the national church and to the state; and a conduct thus rational would at once terminate all the theological differences which now confound the intellects of men, and disseminate universal discord.

The next measure of national improvement should be to repeal or modify those laws which leave the lower orders in ignorance, train them to become intemperate, and produce idleness, gambling, poverty, disease, and murder. The production and consumption of ardent spirits are now legally encouraged; licenses to keepers of gin-shops and unnecessary pot-houses are by thousands annually distributed; the laws of the state now direct those licenses to be distributed; and yet perhaps not one of the authors or guardians of these laws has once reflected how much *each* of those houses daily contributes to public crime, disease, and weakness, or how much they add to the stock of private misery.

Shall we then continue to surround our fellow-creatures with a temptation which, as many of them are now trained, we know they are unable to resist? with a temptation too which predisposes its victims to proceed gradually from a state of temporary insanity, into which they had been led by the example and instruction of those around them, to one of madness and bodily disease, creating more than infantile weakness, which again produces mental torments and horrors, that silently, yet most effectually, undermine every faculty in man which can contribute to private or public happiness?

Can the British Government longer preserve such laws, or countenance a system which trains men to devise and enforce such laws*?

---

* In the year 1736, an act of parliament (stat. 9 Geo. II. c. 23.) was passed. The preamble is as follows: " Whereas the drinking of spirituous liquors or strong waters is become very common, especially amongst the people of lower and inferior rank, the constant and excessive use of which tends greatly to the destruction of their healths, rendering them unfit for useful labour and business, debauching their morals, and inciting them to perpetrate all manner of vices ; and the

Enough surely has been said to exhibit the evil consequences of these laws in their true colours. Let the duties therefore on the production of ardent spirits be gradually increased, until the price shall exceed the means of ordinary consumption ; let the licenses be progressively withdrawn from the present occupiers of gin-shops and unnecessary pot-houses ; and let the duties on the production and consumption of malt liquor be diminished, that the poor and working classes may be the more readily induced to abandon their destructive habits of dram-drinking, and by degrees to withdraw altogether from this incentive to crime, and source of misery.

---

ill consequences of the excessive use of such liquor are not confined to the present generation, but extend to future ages, and tend to the devastation and ruin of this kingdom." It was therefore enacted, that no person should retail spirits without a license, for which £50 was to be paid annually, with other provisions to restrain the sale of spirits. " By a Report of His Majesty's Justices of the Peace for the county of Middlesex, made in January 1736, it appeared that there were then within Westminster, Holborn, the Tower, and Finsbury division, (exclusive of London and Southwark,) 7044 houses and shops wherein spiritous liquors were publicly sold by retail, of which they had got an account, and that they believed it was far short of the true number."

The next improvement should be to discontinue the state lottery.

The law which creates this measure is neither more nor less than a law to legalize gambling, entrap the unwary, and rob the ignorant.

How great must be the error of that system which can induce a state to deceive and injure its subjects, and yet expect that those subjects shall not be necessarily trained to injure and to deceive!

These measures may be thought detrimental to the national revenues.

Those who have reflected on the nature of public revenue, and who possess minds capable of comprehending the subject, know that revenue has but one legitimate source; that it is derived directly or indirectly from the labour of man, and that it may be more or less from any given number of men (other circumstances being similar) in proportion to their strength, industry, and capacity.

The efficient strength of a state governed by laws founded on an accurate knowledge of human nature, in which the whole population are well trained, will greatly exceed one of equal extent and numbers, in which a large part of

the population are improperly trained, and governed by laws founded in ignorance.

Thus were the small states of Greece, while
governed by laws comparatively wise, superior
in national strength to the extended empire of
Persia.

On this plain and obvious principle will the
effective power and resources of the British empire be largely increased by withdrawing those
laws which, under the plausible appearance of
adding a few, and but a few, millions to the an-
nual revenues of this kingdom, in reality feed on
the very vitals of the state. For such laws destroy the energies and capacities of its population, which, so weakened and trained to crime,
requires a far greater expenditure to protect and
govern it.

Confidently may it be said, that a short experience in practice is alone necessary to make the
truth of these positions self-evident even to the
most common understandings.

The next measure for the general improvement of the British population should be to re-
vise the laws relative to the poor. For, pure
and benevolent as, no doubt, were the motives
which actuated those with whom the poor laws
originated, the direct and certain effects of

these laws are to injure the poor, and, through them, the state, as much almost as they can be injured.

They exhibit the appearance of affording aid to the distressed, while, in reality, they prepare the poor to acquire the worst habits, and to practise every kind of crime ; they thus increase the number of the poor, and add to their distress. It becomes therefore necessary that decisive and effectual measures should be adopted to remove those evils which the existing laws have created.

Benevolence says that the destitute must not starve, and to this declaration political wisdom readily assents. Yet can that system be right, which compels the industrious, temperate, and comparatively virtuous, to support the ignorant, the idle, and comparatively vicious? Such however is the effect of the present British poor-laws ; for they publicly proclaim greater encouragement to idleness, ignorance, extravagance, and intemperance, than to industry and good conduct : the evils which arise from a system so irrational, are hourly experienced, and hourly increasing.

It thus becomes necessary that some counteracting remedy be immediately devised and applied ; for, injurious as these laws are, it is obviously impracticable, in the present state of the British population, to annul at once a system to which so large a portion of the people has been taught to look for support.

These laws should be progressively undermined by a system of an opposite nature, and ultimately rendered altogether nugatory.

The proper system to supersede these laws has been in part already explained, but we proceed to unfold it still more. It may be called " A System for the Prevention of Crime, and the Formation of Human Character;" and under an established and well-intentioned government, it will be found more efficacious in producing public benefit than any of the laws now in existence.

The fundamental principle on which all these Essays proceed is, that " Children collectively may be taught any sentiments and habits;" or, in other words, " trained to acquire any character."

It is of importance that *this principle should be ever present in the mind, and that its truth should be established beyond even the shadow of doubt.* To the superficial observer it may appear to be an abstract truth of little value; but to the reflecting and accurate reasoner it will

speedily discover itself to be a power which ulti-
matley must destroy the ignorance, and consequent prejudices, that have accumulated through
all preceding ages.

For as it is a deduction from all the leading
facts in the past history of the world, so it will
be found, on the most extensive investigation, to
be consistent with every fact which now exists.
It is calculated therefore to become the foundation of a new system, which, because true and of
unparalleled importance, must prove irresistible,
will speedily supersede all those which exist, and
itself become permanent.

It is necessary however, prior to the introduction of this system in all its bearings and consequences, that the public mind should be impressed with the deepest conviction of its truth.

For this purpose let us, in imagination, survey
the various states and empires of the world, and
attentively observe man, as in these arbitrary di-
visions of the earth he is known to exist.

Compare the national character of each community with the laws and customs by which they
are respectively governed, and, without an exception, the one will be found the archetype of
the other.

Where, in former ages, the laws and customs

established by Lycurgus formed man into a model for martial exploits, and a perfect instrument for war, he is now trained, by other laws and customs, to be the instrument of a despotism which renders him almost or altogether unfit for war. And where the laws and customs of Athens trained the young mind to acquire as high a degree of partial rationality as the history of preceding times records; man is now reduced, by a total change of laws and customs, to the lowest state of mental degradation. Also where, formerly, the superior native American tribes roamed fearlessly through their trackless forests, uniformly exhibiting the hardy, penetrating, elevated, and sincere character, which was at a loss to comprehend how a rational being could desire to possess more than his nature could enjoy; now, on the very same soil, in the same climate, characters are formed under laws and customs so opposite, that all their bodily and mental faculties are individually exerted to obtain, if possible, ten thousand times more than any man can enjoy.

But why proceed to enumerate such endless results as these, of the never-failing influence of training over human nature, when it may be easily rendered self-evident even to the most illiterate, by daily examples around their own dwellings?

No one, it may be supposed, can now be so defective in knowledge as to imagine that it is a different human nature, which by its own power forms itself into a child of ignorance, of poverty, and of habits leading to crime and to punishment; or into a votary of fashion, claiming distinction from its folly and inconsistency; or to fancy that it is some undefined, blind, unconscious process of human nature itself, distinct from instruction, that forms the sentiments and habits of the men of commerce, of agriculture, the law, the church, the army, the navy, or of the private and illegal depredator on society; or that it is a different human nature which constitutes the societies of the Jews, of Friends, and of all the various religious denominations which have existed or which now exist. No! human nature, save the minute differences which are ever found in all the compounds of the creation, is one and the same in all; it is without exception universally plastic, and, by judicious training, THE INFANTS OF ANY ONE CLASS IN THE WORLD MAY BE READILY FORMED INTO MEN OF ANY OTHER CLASS; EVEN TO BELIEVE AND DECLARE THAT CONDUCT

TO BE RIGHT AND VIRTUOUS, AND TO DIE
IN ITS DEFENCE, WHICH THEIR PARENTS
HAD BEEN TAUGHT TO BELIEVE AND SAY
WAS WRONG AND VICIOUS, AND TO OPPOSE
WHICH, THOSE PARENTS WOULD ALSO HAVE
WILLINGLY SACRIFICED THEIR LIVES.

Whence then the foundation of your claim,
ye advocates for the superiority of the early prepossessions of your sect or party, in opposition
to those taught to other men? Ignorance itself,
at this day, might almost make it evident that
one particle of merit is not due to you for not possessing those notions and habits which you now
the most contemn. Ought you not, and will
you not then, have charity for those who have
been taught different sentiments and habits from
yourselves? Let all men fairly investigate this
subject for themselves; it well merits their most
attentive examination ; they will then discover
that it is from the errors of education, misin-
structing the young mind relative to the true
cause of early prepossessions, that almost all the
evils of life proceed.

Whence then, ye advocates for the merit and
demerit of early prepossessions of opinion, do
you derive your principles?

Let this system of misery be seen in all its

naked deformity! It ought to be so exposed;
for the instruction which it inculcates at the out-
set of forming human character, is destructive of
that genuine charity which can alone train man
to be truly benevolent to all other men. The
ideas of exclusive right and consequent superiority, which men have hitherto been taught to
attach to the early sentiments and habits in which
they have been instructed, are the chief cause of
disunion throughout society; such notions are,
indeed, in direct opposition to pure and undefiled
religion, nor can they ever exist together. The
extent of the misery which they generate cannot
however be much longer concealed; they are
already hastening fast to meet the fate of all
errors; for the gross ignorance on which this
system of misery has been raised, is exposed to
the world on its own proper foundation; and, so
exposed, its supporters will shrink from the task
of defence, and no rational mind will be found
to give it support.

Having exhibited the error on which ignorance
has erected the systems by which man has been
governed, or compelled to become irrational
and miserable; and having laid an immoveable
foundation for a system devoid of that error,
which, when fully comprehended and adopted

into practice, must train mankind " to think of and act to others as they would wish others to think of and act to them,"—we proceed further to explain this *system without error*, and which may be termed a *system without mystery*.

As then children collectively may be formed into any characters, by whom ought their characters to be formed?

The kind and degree of misery or happiness experienced by the members of any community, depend on the characters which have been formed in the individuals which constitute the community. It becomes then the highest interest, and consequently the first and most important duty, of every state, to form the individual characters of which the state is composed. And if any characters, from the most ignorant and miserable to the most rational and happy, can be formed, it surely merits the deepest attention of every state to adopt those means by which the formation of the latter may be secured, and that of the former prevented.

It follows that every state, to be well governed, ought to direct its chief attention to the formation of character; and that the best governed state will be that which shall possess the best national system of education.

Under the guidance of minds competent to its direction, a national system of training and education may be formed, to become the most safe, easy, effectual, and œconomical instrument of government that can be devised. And it may be made to possess a power equal to the accomplishment of the most grand and beneficial purposes.

It is, however, by instruction only that the population of the world can be made conscious of the irrational state in which they now exist; and until, that instruction is given, it is premature to introduce a national system of education.

But the time is now arrived when the British Government may with safety adopt a national system of training and education for the poor and uninstructed; and this measure alone, if the plan shall be well devised and executed, will effect the most importantly beneficial changes.

As a preliminary step, however, it is necessary to observe, that to create a well trained, united, and happy people, this national system should be uniform over the United Kingdom; it should be also founded in the spirit of peace and of rationality; and for the most obvious reasons, the thought of exclusion to one child in the empire should not for a moment be entertained.

Several plans have been lately proposed for the national education of the poor, but these have not been calculated to effect all that a national system for the education of the poor ought to accomplish.

For the authors and supporters of these systems we feel those sentiments which the principles developed throughout these Essays must create in any minds on which they have been early and effectually impressed ; and we are desirous of rendering their labours for the community as extensively beneficial as they can be made. To fulfil, however, a great and important public duty, the plans which they have devised must be considered as though they had been produced and published in the days of antiquity.

The plans alluded to are those of the Reverend Dr. Bell, Mr. Joseph Lancaster, and Mr. Whitbread.

The systems of Dr. Bell and Mr. Lancaster, for instructing the poor in reading, writing, and arithmetic, prove the extreme ignorance which previously existed in the *manner* of training the young ; for it is in the manner alone of giving instruction that these new systems are an improvement on the modes of instruction which were formerly practised.

The arrangement of the room, and many of the details in Mr. Lancaster's plan, are in some respects better calculated to give instruction in the elements enumerated, than those recommended by Dr. Bell, although some of the details introduced by the latter are very superior, and highly deserving of adoption.

The essence, however, of national training and education is to impress on the young, ideas and habits which shall contribute to the future happiness of the individual and of the state; and this can be accomplished only by instructing them to become rational beings.

It must be evident to common observers, that children may be taught, by either Dr. Bell's or Mr. Lancaster's system, to read, write, account, and sew, and yet acquire the worst habits, and have their minds rendered irrational for life.

Reading and writing are merely instruments, by which knowledge, either true or false, may be imparted; and, when given to children, are of little comparative value, unless they are also taught how to make a proper use of them.

When a child receives a full and fair explanation of the objects and characters around him, and when he is also taught to reason correctly, so that he may learn to discover general truths from falsehood; he will be much better instructed, although without the knowledge of one letter or figure, than those are who have been compelled to *believe*, and whose reasoning faculties have been confounded, or destroyed, by what is most erroneously termed learning.

It is readily acknowledged, that the manner of instructing children is of importance, and deserves all the attention which it has lately received; that those who discover or introduce improvements which facilitate the acquirement of knowledge, are important benefactors to their fellow-creatures. Yet the *manner* of giving instruction is one thing, the *instruction* itself another, and no two objects can be more distinct. The *worst* manner may be applied to give the *best* instruction, and the *best* manner to give the *worst* instruction. Were the real importance of both to be estimated by numbers, the manner of instruction may be compared to one, and the matter of instruction to millions; the first is the means only; the last, the end to be accomplished by those means.

If therefore, in a national system of education for the poor, it be desirable to adopt the best *manner*, it is surely so much the more desirable to adopt also the best *matter*, of instruction.

Either give the poor a rational and useful training, or mock not their ignorance, their poverty, and their misery, by merely instructing them to become conscious of the extent of the degradation under which they exist. And therefore, in pity to suffering humanity, either keep the poor, *if you now can*, in the state of the most abject ignorance, as near as possible to animal life ; or at once determine to form them into rational beings, into useful and effective members of the state.

Were it possible, without national prejudice, to examine into the matter of instruction which is now given in some of our boasted new systems for the instruction of the poor, it would be found almost as wretched as any which can be devised. In proof of this statement, enter any one of the schools denominated national, request the master to show the acquirements of the children; these are called out, and he asks them theological questions to which men of the most profound erudition cannot make a rational reply : the children, however, readily answer as they had been previously instructed, for memory in this mockery of learning is all that is required.

Thus the child whose natural faculty of comparing ideas, or whose rational powers, shall be the soonest destroyed, if, at the same time, he possess a memory to retain incongruities without connexion, will become what is termed the first scholar in the class; and three fourths of the time which ought to be devoted to the acquirement of useful instruction, will be really occupied in destroying the mental powers of the children.

To those accustomed attentively to notice the human countenance, from infancy to age, in the various classes and religious denominations of the British population, it is truly an instructive although melancholy employment, to observe in the countenances of the poor children in these schools, the evident expression of mental injury derived from the well intentioned, but most mistaken, plan of their instruction.

It is an important lesson, because it affords another recent and striking example to the millions which previously existed, of the ease with which children may be taught to receive any sectarian notions, and thence acquire any habits, however contrary to their real happiness.

To those trained to become truly conscientious in any of the present sectarian errors which distract the world, this free exposure of the weakness of the peculiar tenets in which such individuals have been instructed, will at first excite feelings of high displeasure and horror; and these feelings will be acute and poignant, in proportion to the obvious and irresistible evidence on which the disclosure of their errors is founded.

Let them, however, begin to think calmly on these subjects, to examine their own minds, and the minds of all around them, and they will become conscious of the absurdities and inconsistencies in which their forefathers have trained them; they will then abhor the errors by which they have been so long abused ; and, with an earnestness not to be resisted, they will exert their utmost faculties to remove the cause of so much misery to man.

Enough surely has now been said of the manner and matter of instruction in these new systems, to exhibit them in a just and true light.

The improvements in the manner of teaching children whatever may be deemed proper for them to learn; improvements which we may easily predict will soon receive great additions and amendments; have proceeded from the Reverend Dr. Bell and Mr. Lancaster; while the errors which their respective systems assist to engrave on the ductile mind of infancy and childhood, are derived from times when ignorance gave countenance to every kind of absurdity.

Mr. Whitbread's scheme for the education of the poor, was evidently the production of an ardent mind possessing considerable abilities: his mind, however, had been irregularly formed by the errors of his early education; and was most conspicuous in the speech which introduced the plan he had devised to the House of Commons, and in the plan itself.

The first was a clear exposition of all the reasons for the education of the poor, which could be expected from a human being trained from infancy under the systems in which Mr. Whitbread had been instructed.

The plan itself evinced the fallacy of the principles which he had imbibed, and showed that he had not acquired a practical knowledge of the feelings and habits of the poor, or of the only effectual means by which they could be trained to be useful to themselves and to the community.

Had Mr. Whitbread not been trained, as almost all the Members of both Houses of Parliament have been, in delusive theories devoid of rational foundation, which prevent them from acquiring an extensive practical knowledge of human nature, he would not have committed a plan for the national education of the poor to the sole management and direction of the Ministers, Churchwardens, and Overseers of Parishes, whose present interests must have appeared to be opposed to the measure.

He would surely first have devised a plan to make it the evident interest of the Ministers, Churchwardens, and Overseers, to co-operate in giving efficacy to the system which he wished to introduce to their superintendence; and also to render them, by previous training, competent to that superintendence for which now they are in general unprepared. For, trained as these individuals have hitherto been, they must be deficient in the practical knowledge necessary to enable them successfully to direct the instruction of others. And had an attempt been made to carry Mr. Whitbread's plan into execution, it would have created a scene of confusion over the whole kingdom.

Attention to the subject will make it evident that it never was, and that it never can be, the interest of any sect claiming exclusive privileges on account of professing high and mysterious doctrines, about which the best and most conscientious men may differ in opinion, that the mass of the people should be otherwise instructed than in those doctrines which were and are in unison with its peculiar tenets; and, that at this hour a national system of education for the lower orders on sound political principles is really dreaded, even by some of the most learned and intelligent members of the church of England. Such feelings in the members of the national church are those only which ought to be expected; for most men so trained and circumstanced must of necessity acquire those feelings. Why therefore should any class of men endeavour to rouse the indignation of the public against them? Their conduct and their motives are equally correct, and therefore equally good with those who raise the cry against and oppose the errors of the church. And let it ever be remembered, that an establishment which possesses the power of propagating principles, may be rendered truly valuable when directed to inculcate a system of self-evident truth, unobstructed by inconsistencies and counteractions.

The Dignitaries of the Church, and their adherents, foresaw that a national system for the education of the poor, unless it were placed under the immediate influence and management of individuals belonging to the church, would effectually and rapidly undermine the errors not only of their own, but of every other ecclesiastical establishment. In this foresight, they evinced the superiority of their penetration over the sectaries by whom the unexclusive system of education is supported. The heads of the church have wisely discovered that reason and inconsistency cannot long exist together; that the one must inevitably destroy the other, and reign paramount. They have witnessed the regular, and latterly the rapid progress which reason has made; they know that its accumulating strength cannot be much longer resisted; and as they now see the contest is hopeless, the unsuccessful attempt to destroy the Lancasterian System of Education is the last effort they will ever make to counteract the dissemination of knowledge, which is now widely extending itself in every direction.

The establishment of the Reverend Dr. Bell's system for initiating the children of the poor in all the tenets of the Church of England, is an attempt to ward off a little longer the yet dreaded period of a change from ignorance to reason; from misery to happiness.

Let us, however, not attempt impossibilities, the task is vain and hopeless ; the church, while it adheres to the defective and injurious parts of its system, cannot be induced to act cordially in opposition to its apparent interests.

The principles here advocated will not admit the application of any deception to any class of men ; they countenance no proceedings in practice, but of unlimited sincerity and candour; they give rise to no one sentiment which is not in unison with the happiness of the human race; and they impart knowledge, which renders it evident that such happiness can never be acquired, until every particle of falsehood and deception shall be eradicated from the instructions which the old force upon the young.

Let us then, in this spirit, openly declare to the church, that a national unexclusive plan of education for the poor will, without the shadow of doubt, destroy all the errors which are attached to the various systems ; and that, when this plan shall be fully established, not one of the tenets which is in opposition to facts can long be upheld.

This unexclusive system for the education of the poor has gone forth ; and having found a resting-place in the minds of its supporters, it will never more return even to the control of its projectors ; but it will be speedily so improved, that by rapidly increasing strides it will firmly establish the reign of reason and happiness.

Seeing and knowing this, let us also make it equally evident to the church,—warn it of its actual state,—cordially and sincerely assist its members quietly to withdraw those inconsistencies from the system, which now create its weakness and its danger ; that it may retain those rational principles alone which can be successfully defended against attack, or which rather will prevent any attack from being attempted, or even meditated.

The wise and prudent then of all parties, instead of wishing to destroy national establishments, will use their utmost exertions to render them so consistent and reasonable in all their parts, that every well-disposed mind may be induced to give them their hearty and willing support.

For the first grand step towards effecting any substantial improvement in these realms, without injury to any part of the community, is to make it the clear and decided interest of the church to co-operate cordially in all the projected ameliorations. Once found a national church on the true, unlimited, and genuine principles of mental charity, and all the members of the state will soon improve in every truly valuable quality. If the temperate and discerning of all parties will not now lend their aid to effect this change by peaceable means,—which may with the greatest ease and with unerring certainty be done,—it is evident, to every calm observer, that the struggle by those who now exist in unnecessary misery to obtain that degree of happiness which they may attain in practice, cannot long be deferred. It will therefore prove true political wisdom to anticipate and guide these feelings.

To those who can reflect, and will attend to the passing scenes before them, the times are indeed awfully interesting ; some change of high import, scarcely yet perhaps to be scanned by the present ill-taught race of men, is evidently in progress : in consequence, well founded, prompt, and decisive measures are now required in the British councils, to direct this change, and relieve the nation from the errors of its present systems.

It must surely then be the desire of every rational man, of every true friend to humanity, that a cordial co-operation and unity of action should be effected between the British Executive, the Parliament, the Church, and the People, to lay a broad and firm foundation for the future happiness of themselves and the world.

Say not, my countrymen, that such an event is impracticable; for, by adopting the evident means to form a rational character in man, there is a plain and direct road opened, which, if pursued, will render its accomplishment not only possible but certain. That road too will be found the most safe and pleasant that human beings have ever yet travelled. It leads direct to intelligence and true knowledge, and will show the boasted acquirements of Greece, of Rome, and of all antiquity, to be the mere weakness of mental infancy. Those who travel this road will find it so straight and well defined, that no one will be in danger of wandering from the right course. Nor is it yet a narrow or exclusive path; it admits of no exclusion, every colour of body and diversity of mind are freely and alike admitted. It is open to the human race, and it is broad and spacious enough to receive the whole, were they increased a thousand fold.

We well know that a declaration like the one now made, must sound chimerical in the ears of those who have hitherto wandered in the dark mazes of ignorance, error, and exclusion; and who have been taught folly and inconsistencies only, from their cradle. But if every known fact connected with the subject proves that, from the day in which man first saw light to that in which the sun now shines, the old collectively have taught the young collectively the sentiments and habits which the young have acquired; and that the present generation, and every following generation, must in like manner instruct their successors; then do we say, with a confidence founded on certainty itself, that even much more shall come to pass than has yet been foretold, or promised. When these principles, derived from the unchangeable laws of nature, and equally revealed to all men, shall, as they soon will, be publicly established in the world, no conceivable obstacle can remain to prevent a sincere and cordial union and co-operation for every wise and good purpose, not only among all the members of the same state, but also among the rulers of those kingdoms and empires whose enmity and rancour against each other have been carried to the utmost stretch of melancholy folly, and even occasionally to a high degree of madness.

Such, my fellow-men, are some, and yet but a few, of the mighty consequences which must result from the public acknowledgement of these plain, simple, and irresistible truths. They will not prove a delusive promise of mockery, but will in reality speedily and effectually establish peace, good-will, and an ever-active benevolence throughout the whole human race.

The public avowal of these principles, and their general introduction into practice, will constitute that invaluable secret, for which the human mind, from its birth, has been in perpetual search; its future beneficial consequences no man can yet foresee.

We will now show how these principles may be immediately and most advantageously introduced into general practice.

It has been said that "the state which shall possess the best national system of education, will be the best governed;" and if the principle on which all the reasoning of these Essays is founded, be true, then is that sentiment also true. Yet (will future ages credit the fact?) to this day the British Government is without any national system of training and education, even for its millions of poor and uninstructed!! The formation of the mind and habits of its subjects is permitted to go on at random, often in the hands of those who are the most incompetent in the empire ; and the result is, the gross ignorance and disunion which now every where abound*!!

Instead of continuing such unwise proceedings, a national system for the training and education of the labouring classes ought to be immediately arranged; and, if judiciously devised, it may be rendered the most valuable improvement ever yet introduced into practice.

For this purpose, an act should be passed for the instruction of all the poor and labouring classes in the three kingdoms.

In this act provision should be made,

First,—For the appointment of proper persons to direct this new department of Government, which will be found ultimately to prove the most important of all its departments : consequently, those individuals who possess the highest integrity, abilities, and influence in the state, should be appointed to its direction.

---

* Even the recent attempts which have been made are conducted on the narrow principle of debasing man to a mere irrational military machine, which is to be rapidly moved by animal force.

Second,—For the establishment of seminaries, in which those individuals, who shall be destined to form the minds and bodies of the future subjects of these realms, should be well initiated in the art and matter of instruction.

This is, and ought to be considered, an office of the greatest practical trust and confidence in the empire; for let this duty be well performed, and the government must proceed with ease to the people, and high gratification to those who govern.

At present, there are not any individuals in the kingdom who have been trained to instruct the rising generation, as it is for the interest and happiness of all that it should be instructed. The training of those who are to form the future man becomes a consideration of the utmost magnitude: for, on due reflection, it will appear that instruction to the young must be, of necessity, the only foundation upon which the superstructure of society can be raised. Let this instruction continue to be left, as heretofore, to chance, and often to the most inefficient members of the community, and society must still experience the endless miseries which arise from such weak and puerile conduct. On the contrary, let the instruction to the young be well devised and well executed, and no subsequent proceedings in the state can be materially injurious. For it may truly be said to be a wonder-working power; one that merits the deepest attention of the legislature; with ease it may be used to train man into a dæmon of mischief to himself and all around him, or into an agent of unlimited benevolence.

Third,—For the establishment of seminaries over the United Kingdoms; to be conveniently placed, and of sufficient extent to receive all those who require instruction.

Fourth,—For supplying the requisite expenditure for the building and support of those seminaries.

Fifth,—For their arrangement on the plan, which, for the manner of instruction, upon a due comparison of the various modes now in practice, or which may be devised, shall appear to be the best.

Sixth,—For the appointment of proper masters to each of the schools. And,

Last,—The matter of instruction, both for body and mind, in these seminaries, should be substantially beneficial to the individuals, and to the state. For this is, or ought to be, the sole motive for the establishment of national seminaries.

These are the outlines of the provisions necessary to prepare the most powerful instrument of good that has ever yet been placed in the hands of man.

The last national improvement which remains to be proposed, in the present state of the public mind, is, that another legislative act should be passed, for the purpose of obtaining regular and accurate information relative to the value of and demand for labour, over the United Kingdoms. This information is necessary, preparatory to the adoption of measures which will be proposed, to provide labour for those who may be occasionally unable to procure other employment.

In this act, provision should be made,

First,—To obtain accurate quarterly returns of the state of labour in each county, or smaller district; the returns to be made either by the clergy, justices of the peace, or other more competent persons. These returns should contain,

First,—The average price of manual labour within the district, for the period included in the return.

Second,—The number of those in each district who depend on their daily labour, or the parish, for their support; and who may be at the period of these returns unemployed, and yet able to labour.

Third,—The number of those who, at the period of each return, are but partially employed; and the extent of that partial employment.

Provision should also be made to obtain a statement of the general occupations in which the individuals had been formerly employed, with the best conjectures as to the kind and quantity of work which each may be supposed still capable of performing.

The want of due attention to this highly necessary branch of government, occasions thousands of our fellow subjects to be made wretched; while, from the same cause, the revenues of the empire are annually deteriorated to an enormous amount.

We have stated, because it is easy of proof, that the revenues of all countries are derived, directly or indirectly, from the labour of man; and yet the British Government, which, with all its errors, is among the best devised and most enlightened that have hitherto been established, makes extravagant and unnecessary waste of that labour.   It makes this waste too in the midst of its greatest pecuniary difficulties, and when the utmost efforts of every individual in the state are requisite!

This waste of human labour, as it is highly unjust to all, is not only impolitic in a national view, but it is most cruel to the individuals who, in consequence of this waste, are the immediate sufferers.

It would be an Herculean task to trace through all their ramifications the various injurious effects which result from the fundamental errors by which man has been, and is governed ; nor is the world yet fully prepared for such development. We shall therefore now merely sketch some of the most direct and palpable of these effects, relative to the oversight of governments in regard to the non-application or mis-application of the labour of the poor and unoccupied.

It has been shown that the governing powers of any country may easily and œconomically give its subjects just sentiments, and the best habits ; and so long as this shall remain unattempted, governments will continue to neglect their most important duties, as well as interests. Such neglect now exists in Britain, where, in lieu of the governing powers making any effort to attain these inestimable benefits for the individuals belonging to the empire, they content themselves with the existence of laws, which must create sentiments and habits highly injurious to the welfare of the individuals and of the state.

Many of these laws, by their never-failing ef-

fects, speak in a language which no one can misunderstand; and say to the unprotected and untaught, *Remain in ignorance, and let your labour be directed by that ignorance: for while
you can procure what is sufficient to support life
by such labour, although that life should be an
existence in abject poverty, disease, and misery,
we will not trouble ourselves with you, or any of
your proceedings: when, however, you can no
longer procure work, or obtain the means to
support nature, then apply for relief to the parish; and you shall be maintained in idleness.*

And in ignorance and idleness, even in this
country, where manual labour is or always might
be made valuable, hundreds of thousands of
men, women, and children, are daily supported.
No one acquainted with human nature will suppose that men, women, and children, can be long
maintained in ignorance and idleness, without
becoming habituated to crime*.

---

* It would perhaps prove an interesting calculation, and useful to a government, to estimate how much its finances would
be improved by giving proper employment to a million of its
subjects, rather than by supporting that million in ignorance,
idleness, and crime.

Will it exceed the bounds of moderation to say, that a million of the population so employed, under the direction of an
intelligent government, might earn to the state ten pounds
each annually, or ten millions sterling per annum? Ten mil-

Why then are there any idle poor in these kingdoms? Solely because so large a part of the population have been permitted to grow up to manhood in gross ignorance; and because, when they are, or easily may be, trained to be willing to labour, useful and productive employment has not been provided for them.

All men may, by judicious and proper laws and training, readily acquire knowledge and habits which will enable them, if they be permitted, to produce far more than they need for their support and enjoyment; and thus any population, in the fertile parts of the earth, may be taught to live in plenty and in happiness, without the checks of vice and misery.

Mr. Malthus is however correct, when he says that the population of the world is ever adapting itself to the quantity of food raised for its support; but he has not told us how much more food an intelligent and industrious people will create from the same soil, than will be produced by one ignorant and ill-governed. It is however as one, to infinity.

---

lions per year would be obtained by each individual earning less than four shillings per week; and any part of the population of these kingdoms, including within the average the too young and the too old for labour, may be made to earn, under proper arrangements, more than four shillings per week to the state, besides creating an innumerable train of other more beneficial consequences.

For man knows not the limit to his power of creating food. How much has this power been latterly increased in these islands! And in them such knowledge is in its infancy. Yet compare even this power of raising food with the efforts of the Bosgemens or other savages, and it will be found perhaps as one, to a thousand.

Food for man may be also considered as a compound of the original elements; of the qualities, combinations, and control of which, chemistry is daily adding to our knowledge; nor is it *yet* for man to say to what this knowledge may lead, or where it may end.

The sea, it may be remarked also, affords an inexhaustible source of food. It may then be safely asserted, that the population of the world may be allowed naturally to increase for many thousand years; and yet, under a system of government founded on the principles for the truth of which we contend, the whole may continue to live, in abundance and happiness, without one check of vice or of misery; and, under the guidance of these principles, human labour, properly directed, may be made far more than sufficient to enable the population of the world to live in the highest state of human enjoyment.

Shall we then continue to allow misery to preominate, and the labour of man to be most absurdly applied or wasted, when it might be easily directed to remove that misery?

The labour of every man, woman, and child, possessing sufficient bodily strength, may be advantageously employed for the public; and there is not perhaps a stronger evidence of the extreme ignorance and fallacy of the systems which have hitherto governed the world, than that the rich, the active, and the powerful, should, by tacit consent, support the ignorant in idleness and crime, without making the attempt to train them into industrious, intelligent, and valuable members of the community; although the means by which the change could be easily effected have been always at their command!

It is not, however, intended to propose that the British Government should now give direct employment to all its working population: on the contrary, it is confidently expected that a national system for the training and education of the poor, and lower orders, will be so effectual, that ere long they will all find employment sufficient to support themselves, except in cases of a great sudden depression in the demand for, and consequent depreciation in the value of, labour.

To prevent the crime and misery which ever follow these unfavourable fluctuations in the demand for and value of labour, it ought to be a primary duty of every government that sincerely interests itself in the well-being of its subjects, to provide perpetual employment of real national utility, in which all who apply may be immediately occupied.

In order that those only who could not obtain employment from private individuals should be induced to avail themselves of these national works, the rate of the public labour might be in general fixed at some proportion less than the average rate of private labour in the district in which such public labour should be performed. These rates might be readily ascertained and fixed, by reference to the county or district quarterly returns of the average rate of labour.

This measure, judiciously managed, would have a similar effect on the price of labour, that the sinking fund produces on the Stock Exchange; and, as the price of public labour should never fall below the means of temperate existence, the plan proposed would perpetually tend to prevent an excess of nationally injurious pressure on the most unprotected part of society.

The most obvious, and in the first place the best, source perhaps of employment would be the making and repairing of roads. Such employment would be perpetual over the whole kingdom; and it will be found true national œconomy to keep the public roads at all times in a much higher state of repair than perhaps any of them are at present. If requisite, canals, harbours, docks, ship-building, and materials for the navy, may be afterwards resorted to: it is not, however, supposed that many of the latter resources would be necessary.

A persevering attention, without which indeed not any thing beneficial in practice can ever be attained, will soon overcome all the difficulties which may at first appear to obstruct this plan for introducing occasional national employment into the polity of the kingdom.

In times of very limited demand for labour, it is truly lamentable to witness the distress which arises among the industrious for want of regular employment, and their customary wages. In these periods, innumerable applications are made to the Superintendants of extensive manual operations, to obtain any kind of employment by which a subsistence may be procured. Such applications are often made by persons who, in search of work, have travelled from one extremity of the island to the other!

During these attempts to be useful and honest, in the common acceptation of the terms, the families of such wandering individuals accompany them, or remain at home; in either case, they generally experience sufferings and privations which the gay and splendid will hesitate to believe it possible that human nature could endure.

Yet, after this extended and anxious endeavour to procure employment, the applicant often returns unsuccessful; he cannot, by his most strenuous exertions, procure an honest and independent existence: therefore, with intentions perhaps as good, and a mind as capable of great and benevolent actions as the remainder of his fellow men, he has no other resources left but to starve; apply to his parish for relief, and thus suffer the greatest degradation; or rely on his own native exertions, and, to supply himself and family with bread, resort to what are termed dishonest means.

Some minds thus circumstanced are so delicately formed, that they will not accept the one, or adopt the other of the two latter modes to sustain life, and in consequence they actually starve. These, however, it is to be hoped, are not very numerous. But the number is undoubtedly great, of those whose health is ruined by bad and insufficient food, clothing, and shelter; who contract lingering diseases, and suffer premature death, the effect of partial starvation.

The most ignorant and least enterprising of them apply to the parish for support; soon lose the desire of exertion; become permanently dependent; conscious of their degradation in society; and henceforward, with their offspring, remain a burden and grievous evil to the state; while those among this class who yet possess strength and energy of body and mind, with some undestroyed powers of reasoning, perceive, in part, the glaring errors and injustice of society towards themselves and their fellow sufferers.

Can it then create surprise that feelings like those described should force human nature to endeavour to retaliate?

Multitudes of our fellow men are so goaded by these reflections and circumstances, as to be urged, even while incessantly and closely pursued by legal death, almost without a chance of escape, to resist those laws under which they suffer; and thus the private depredator on society is formed, fostered, and matured.

Shall we then longer withhold national instruction from our fellow men, who, it has been shown, might easily be trained to be industrious, intelligent, virtuous, and valuable members of the state?

True indeed it is, that all the measures now proposed are only a compromise with the errors of the present systems: but as these errors now almost universally exist, and must be overcome solely by the force of reason; and as reason, to effect the most beneficial purposes, makes her advance by slow degrees, and progressively substantiates one truth of high import after another, it will be evident to minds of comprehensive and accurate thought, that by these and similar compromises alone can success be rationally expected in practice. For such compromises bring truth and error before the pub lic; and whenever they are fairly exhibited together, truth must ultimately prevail.

As many of the inconsistencies of the present systems are evident to the most intelligent and well disposed minds, the way for the public admission of the important truths which have now been in part unfolded*, seems to be rendered easy; and it is confidently expected that the period is at hand, when man through ignorance shall not much longer inflict unnecessary misery on man : because, the mass of mankind will become enlightened, and clearly discern that by so acting they will inevitably create misery to themselves. For the extensive knowledge of the facts which present themselves on the globe, makes it evident to those whose rea-

---

* As soon as the public mind shall be sufficiently prepared to receive it, the practical detail of this system shall be fully developed.

soning faculties have not been entirely paralysed, that all mankind firmly believe, that every body, except themselves, has been grievously deceived in his fundamental principles; and feel the utmost astonishment that the nations of the world could embrace such gross inconsistencies for divine or political truths. Most persons are now also prepared to understand that these weaknesses are firmly and conscientiously fixed in the minds of millions, who, when born, possessed equal faculties with themselves. And although they plainly discern in others what they deem inconceivable aberrations of the mental powers, yet, in despite of such facts, they are taught to believe *that they themselves could not have been so deceived;* and this impression is made upon the infant mind with the greatest ease, whether it be to create followers of the most ignorant, or of the most enlightened systems.

The inhabitants of the world are therefore abundantly conscious of the inconsistencies contained in those systems in which all have been trained, out of the pale of their own peculiar, and, as they are taught to believe, highly favoured sect: and yet, the number of the largest sect in the world is small, when compared with the remaining sects, which have been instructed to think the notions of that larger division an error of the grossest kind ; proceeding alone from the ignorance or deception of their predecessors.

All that is now requisite, previous to withdrawing the last mental bandage by which, hitherto, the human race has been kept in darkness and misery, is, by calm and patient reasoning to tranquillize the public mind ; and thus to prevent the evil effects which otherwise might arise from the too sudden prospect of freely enjoying rational liberty of mind.

To withdraw that bandage without danger, reason must be judiciously applied to lead men of every sect (for all have been in part abused) to reflect, that if untold myriads of beings, formed like themselves, have been so grossly deceived as they believe them to have been, what power in nature was there to prevent *them* from being equally deceived ?

Such reflections, steadily pursued by those who are anxious to follow the plain and simple path of reason, will soon make it obvious that the inconsistencies which they behold in all other sects *out of their own pale*, are precisely similar to those which all other sects can readily discover *within that pale.*

It is not however to be imagined, that this

free and open exposure of the gross errors in which the existing generation has been instructed should be forthwith palatable to the world ; it would be contrary to reason to form any such expectations.

Yet, as evil exists, and as man cannot be rational, nor of course happy, until the cause, of it shall be removed ; the writer, like a physician who feels the deepest interest in the welfare of his patient, has hitherto administered of this unpalatable restorative the smallest quantity which he deemed sufficient for the purpose: he now waits to see the effects which that may produce : should the application not prove of sufficient strength to remove the mental disorder, he promises that it shall be increased, until sound health to the public mind be firmly and permanently established.

THE END.